IPS

Feeding the Few: Corporate Control of Food

Susan George

Published by the Institute for Policy Studies.

Copies of this book are available from the Institute for Policy Studies,
1901 Q Street, N.W., Washington, D.C. 20009 or The Transnational
Institute, Paulus Potterstraat 20, 1071 DA, Amsterdam, Holland.

First Printing, 1979
Second Printing, 1981

ISBN 0-89758-010-9

About the Author

Susan George was graduated from Smith College, where she was elected to Phi Beta Kappa, and received a "Licence" in philosophy from the Sorbonne. She recently completed a doctorate at the Ecole des Hautes Etudes en Sciences Sociales of the University of Paris where her thesis was awarded a "Mention Trés Bien.". She was an active militant in the anti-Vietnam-war struggle and has been a Fellow of the Transnational Institute since it was founded in 1973. She participated in preparing the TNI counter-report for the World Food Conference, *World Hunger: Causes and Remedies.* Her subsequent work on food issues led to publication in 1976 of her book, *How the Other Half Dies: The Real Reasons for World Hunger,* which has been reprinted several times in the US and Great Britain and translated into numerous foreign languages. She is currently at work on another book about rural development, requested by her British publishers. Susan George lives in Paris, is married and has three children.

Contents

AUTHOR'S FOREWORD

PART I   THE NEW INTERNATIONAL ECONOMIC
         ORDER: WHO WOULD BENEFIT? 1
  The NIEO and Development Choices............2
  Money Isn't Everything 9

PART II NIEO: THE NEW IMPERIALIST
         ECONOMIC ORDER 21
  Firms and Farms: The US Food System 23
  Vertical Integration 28
  Agribusiness Goes Abroad 32
  Agribusiness Upstream From the
  Third World Farm 35
  Wiring the Third World Farm Into One
  World Market 44
  You Take the Risks, I'll Take the Profits........48
  Agribusiness Downstream from the Third
  World Farm: Anything They Can Do We
  Can Do Better.............................55
  New Weapons in the Grain Arsenal 56
  Post Harvest Technology 59
  Change Their Tastes, Change Their Minds 63

NOTES TOWARD A CONCLUSION 66
GLOSSARY 71
APPENDIX 72
REFERENCES PART I 74
REFERENCES PART II 75

Author's Foreword

This study is a contribution to the Transnational Institute's International Economic Order Project directed by Howard M. Wachtel. It is an attempt to place issues concerning food and agricultural commodities in the context of changing world economic relationships. The first part deals with what the Third World is asking for; the second with what, in my view, it is actually getting. As one discussion after another on agricultural raw materials ends in stalemate, new kinds of food systems are meanwhile introduced in underdeveloped countries by the powerful nations of the North, led by the USA. The study is intended, however, less to provide answers than to suggest a critical perspective and perhaps some new tools for analysis of the ongoing takeover of Third World food systems, designed in the image of the developed countries and for their benefit.

Since many readers of this study and of my book will of necessity be the same people, I have taken what I hope are sufficient pains not to bore them by using a different approach here and by not incorporating examples, data, etc. previously published (at least not by me!). This may result in some unevenness, and I have occasionally resorted to noting that certain important matters are better covered in the book than in this shorter study. Readers interested in my fuller views on the food problem (which have altered only marginally since 1976-77) will find *How the Other Half Dies* available in the United States through Allanheld, Osmun & Co., 19 Brunswick Road, Montclair, New Jersey 07042 (at $4.95 in paperback and $12.50 in hardback) and in the United Kingdom and Canada through Penguin Books (as a Pelican Original).

I am most grateful to my colleagues at TNI, Eleanor LeCain and Howard M. Wachtel, as well as to Claude Bourdet, Harris Gleckman, Sylvain Minault and Pierre Spitz; all of whom took the time and trouble to contribute their extremely helpful suggestions for improving this study.

PART I

The New International Economic Order: Who Would Benefit?

Along with energy and the arms race, food is certainly one of the crucial political problems of the remainder of the twentieth century. Assuming that we do not manage to blow up the planet in the next twenty-five years or so, and that growing awareness of the scarcity of non-renewable resources leads to decisive action on alternate and safe sources of energy, food may indeed be *the* issue that shapes our economic and political future. Who grows food—and how much; who eats it—and at what cost—are questions that will determine social and political relationships not only inside the boundaries of individual nations but also between countries at the international level. When, for example, Egypt increases the price of basic food-stuffs, riots immediately break out, imperiling the government which retaliates with military force. Other governments with chronic food shortages risk imminent collapse in the absence of outside aid. And with the aid come directives from the donors as to what measures the recipients must take to put their political houses in order. Meanwhile, even pretenses of "development" founder in countries where large percentages of the population are in no position to grow enough or to buy enough food to meet their fundamental physiological needs. Food dependency conditions other kinds of dependency, and so long as a nation has failed to solve its own food problem, there is little chance that it can practice any truly independent policies, whether domestic or foreign.

Ever since OPEC's arrival in the foreground of the international scene, a new mood of militancy has taken hold in the underdeveloped countries (UDCs) and calls for a New International Economic Order (NIEO) have become more vigorous. Nineteen seventy-six was an especially important year, marked by the Third Ministerial Meeting of the Third World in Manila, the fourth United Nations Conference on Trade and Development (UNCTAD) meeting in Nairobi, and the Conference baptised "North-South Dialogue" (CIEC) in Paris.[1]

The NIEO, as seen from the Southern hemisphere, is about economic justice on a world scale, to be achieved through more favorable, stable and guaranteed prices for the UDCs' major exports;

together with equally important measures such as a larger share of the world's industrial capacity, debt relief, increased aid, indexation of the prices of primary commodities to those of industrial goods and greater access to Northern industrial markets. The NIEO has been fully defined by the UN General Assembly's sixth and seventh Special Sessions; while the basic Third World demands have been elaborated by UNCTAD over the years and stated most concisely in the Manila Declaration and Program of Action (February 1976), drafted by the representatives of the UDC's "Group of 77" which now includes over a hundred Third World States.

Whatever the total package of measures that should ideally make up the NIEO, the only serious negotiations to date have concerned an Integrated Commodities Program, meaning producer-consumer agreements to hold stocks of the principal commodities and to keep their prices within predetermined limits; as well as a $6 billion Common Fund to finance the stockpiles. Whereas UNCTAD has recommended that eighteen primary products make up the Integrated ' Commodities Program; in fact, only ten have actually come under discussion. They are referred to as the "core commodities" and eight of them are agricultural products or foodstuffs. The list of ten is: coffee, tea, cocoa, sugar, cotton, jute, rubber, hard fibres, copper and tin.

The industrialized nations unfortunately tend to become excited about commodities only when prices are high. When prices stabilize or fall, they revert to their customary foot-dragging behavior at negotiating conferences and this has prevented any serious progress from taking place. In this regard, Germany and Japan are as tough customers for the Third World as the US. The latest round of negotiations (April 1978) ended in failure. There are, however, signs that some concessions may be made to Third World claims in a relatively short term future.

The NIEO and Development Choices

We must recognize that most UDCs are at present highly dependent on revenue from exports of primary products and we should therefore defend their demands for fairer prices and stabilized world markets. This being said, we owe to ourselves and to those who are struggling in the Third World for greater social and political justice a critical examination of what the NIEO may mean. Which social classes in the UDCs would most benefit from it? What are its prospects for fostering real development? To what degree might the acceptance of certain UDC proposals by the wealthy nations actually result in *greater manipulation and dependency* of the poor countries? And while the industrialized North is allowing the peripheral South to talk itself to death in Dialogue after Special Session after International Conference, what *other* NIEO in the realm of food and agriculture is being surreptitiously introduced into the UDCs? These are some of the questions we shall try to address.

The "package-deal" NIEO has not really been taken seriously by the North and all the talks to date have revolved around export incomes from primary products—which boils down to renovating the "export-led" development strategy. Third World negotiators may not be happy about it, but for the moment they are boxed into putting these particular items first on the agenda. There is, in fact, *no* agenda for negotiating the other measures that ought normally to make up the NIEO. So export-led development strategy it is, like it or not.

Let us assume this strategy succeeds, that the industrialized countries recognize the demands of the Third World (those on the current agenda) and that suddenly an Integrated Commodities Program and a Common Fund become realities. This is not an entirely gratuitous hypothesis, and in the middle term may even be a likely one. We are no longer living in the age of cave-man capitalism. The Director of the US National Commission on Supplies and Shortages recently reported on his discussions with executives of companies and described "a new concern on their part for stability and continuity of supply (of Third World raw materials)—even if it means they must pay higher prices."[2]*

The Trilateral Commission and Zbigniew Brzezinski have come out for "a more forward attitude" towards the demands of the Third World—even though this attitude has not yet been much in evidence in the US negotiating stance. The more sophisticated spokespeople for a renovated capitalist economic order must of course contend with the dinosaurs who see the unchecked activities of the "market" as the best allocator of resources. But it is possible that one day certain facts may filter through, even to the dinosaurs, and the facts indicate that the United States has a good deal to gain from acceding to these particular demands of the "77."

A distinguished American economist has, for example, concluded after detailed study that "important benefits would accrue to .

*A spokesman for the London Metals Exchange (LME), "*the* world market for major metals" (including NIEO core commodities copper and tin) expects implementation of UNCTAD's buffer stock/Common Fund program "in about three or four years' time." He says, "I don't think the LME would be the slightest bit perturbed at the idea of a buffer stock system being set up," for the excellent reason that the Exchange would very likely manage it. See Geoffrey Smith, "Contangos, Backwardation and Other Dangerous Games," *Forbes*, 3 April 1978.

3

. . industrial countries from price stabilization." In the United States alone, had stable commodity prices been instituted ten years ago, the economic gains for Americans (in prevented unemployment and GNP loss) would have amounted to "about $15 billion over the decade." For the same period, incremental income to UDC exporters of the core commodities would have been only about $5 billion—or three times less. Moreover, such gains could be had without aggravating inflation. Depending on how one calculates, it would take price increases for core commodities of 30% to 200% to cause even a 1% increase in the US consumer price index. Such figures are vastly above what the UDCs are actually calling for. The buffer stock scheme would even reduce inflationary pressures and this argument may well be the clincher in the US government's attitude:

> The really large gainers from international commodity stabilization programs may be the residents of the developed countries due to the amelioration of inflationary pressures. In the United States, the government is placing increasing emphasis on these gains in explaining its recent greater receptivity to the possibility of instituting new international commodity agreements.[3]

Western governments may thus have a very real interest in promoting price stabilization on a world scale. More difficult to gauge precisely is the attitude of multinational corporations (MNCs) who, although they do not sit at the negotiating tables, are nonetheless heeded by those who do; their preferences may be crucial to the outcome of international talks. On the one hand, the firms which are the major users of the core commodities want stability, as risk-free a business climate as possible, and above all, predictability. They would probably prefer anything, including higher costs (to be passed along to the consumer anyway), to the establishment of effective OPEC-type cartels for primary products. But on the other hand, MNCs are certainly in the best position to profit from present fluctuations on international commodity markets and they possess the necessary information networks that enable them to take immediate advantage of particular situations. If a given country is desperate for foreign exchange and willing to sell its core commodity at bargain-basement prices, an MNC is not going to refuse. So-called "world" prices for commodities are frequently mythical and set after-the-fact; they may hide a huge number of special cases and the kinds of price heterogeneity that well-managed firms will seize upon. Price stabilization would eliminate some of the unpredictability from doing business, but it would simultaneously eliminate some of the more exciting opportunities for making *coups*.

One cannot therefore flatly state that there will be a noticeable shift in US policy towards the NIEO, insofar as this policy is deter-

4

mined by multinationals. Things are presently (September 1978) quiet on the North-South front. Predictions are especially dangerous, as the man said, when they concern the future. Still it seems reasonable to suppose that when higher commodity prices or Third World political pressures result in serious negotiating, the industrialized countries' stance may chance.

Naturally, there would be some advantages to UDCs (or at least to their upper classes) in wresting from the North even a truncated NIEO. Negotiators for the "77" do not, however, always appear fully aware of the disadvantages, and they do not generally object to the class structures in their own societies which prevent equitable distribution of whatever wealth there is. Put more bluntly, and assuming higher revenues for these exporting nations, who, exactly, is likely to see the money? In the most common instance, not the producers who do most of the work to supply the commodities. If we take a look at data on pie-sharing in Third World core commodity-producing countries, we find, for example, that in the Ivory Coast—a major coffee and cocoa exporter—the top 5% of the population receives 30% of the national income, while the bottom fifth of the population gets 4%. In Brazil (coffee and sugar exports) the figures are respectively 27% for the wealthiest 5% and 5% for the poorest 20%; in Malaysia (rubber) 28% for the top and only 3.4% for the bottom; in the Dominican Republic (sugar) 26% and 5%, etc. A comparison with developed capitalist countries shows that in the USA the top 5% of the population receives 13.3% of the national income and the bottom 20% gets 6.7%; in Canada it is 14% and 6.4%.[4]

People who believe in the "trickle-down" theory of development may claim that higher national incomes will eventually benefit the worst off, but even a modest knowledge of the past shows that upper classes do not cheerfully share their privileges—indeed one wonders why anyone should expect them to do so if not forced. Nor do they (in most UDCs) spend their revenues on employment generating activities but prefer speculation, Swiss bank accounts and conspicuous consumption of imported luxuries to productive investment in their own countries.

Furthermore, there are several large and densely populated countries (especially in Asia) for whom the proposed commodity agreements would make little difference, since 20% or less of their exports are made up of the core commodities. Such nations as Burma, India, Indonesia and Pakistan—all classed by the World Bank as among the poorest—would benefit relatively little from such programs.

Countries that stand to gain the most—those whose exports are made up of 70% or more of the ten core commodities—are Bangladesh, Sri Lanka, Zambia, Zaire, Chile and Uganda (plus a smattering of very small ones like Mauritius and Rwanda).[5] One is led to ask if

5

Pie-Sharing in Third World Core Commodity Exporting Countries

IVORY COAST

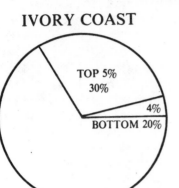

TOP 5%
30%

4%
BOTTOM 20%

NATIONAL INCOME

BRAZIL

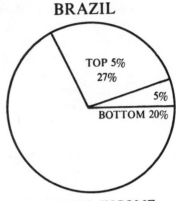

TOP 5%
27%

5%
BOTTOM 20%

NATIONAL INCOME

MALAYSIA

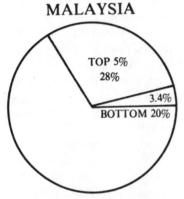

TOP 5%
28%

3.4%
BOTTOM 20%

NATIONAL INCOME

DOMINICAN REPUBLIC

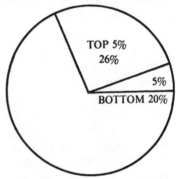

TOP 5%
26%

5%
BOTTOM 20%

NATIONAL INCOME

USA

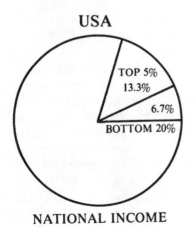

TOP 5%
13.3%

6.7%
BOTTOM 20%

NATIONAL INCOME

CANADA

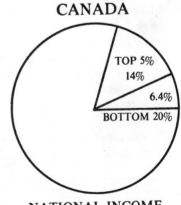

TOP 5%
14%

6.4%
BOTTOM 20%

NATIONAL INCOME

higher revenues for Mobutu, Pinochet and Idi Amin Dada should be priorities for the international community. There are, of course, countries where increased export revenues would doubtless be used to better the conditions of the people as a whole; the examples of Tanzania and Jamaica come to mind. Nor should one exclude the possibility of revolutionary change in others where singularly unjust class structures prevail today.

Still, there are reservations to be made concerning the NIEO on grounds of gross inequalities of distribution inside many Third World societies, on grounds of the repressive nature of several governments that would most benefit and because the scheme as it stands would leave many nations out in the cold. Commodities trading is not, however, the best area in which to envisage or apply political sanctions and these reservations do not imply that there should *not* be fairer prices for raw materials—simply that *of themselves* such adjustments would certainly not erase the problems of poverty and underdevelopment.

Since the eradication of poverty and underdevelopment has not proved to date of overriding concern to the industrialized countries, they are not likely to hesitate if they see, individually or collectively, their economic or geopolitical interest in acceding to certain Third World demands. The United States, for example, may well have noticed that European countries and Japan would bear most of the financial burden of a Common Fund since they import over five times as many commodities from the Third World as does the United States.[6] But since these same Third World countries are also important *customers* for Europe, the latter should encourage higher revenues for commodities, revenues which can be pumped back into the EEC economies. The same argument applies to America which now sends about 27% of its exports to non-oil producing UDCs. If the latter are to continue to pay for these goods, they must have incomes from their own exports.

There must be a two-way street in trade not only to enable the Third World to remain a paying customer for the industrialized countries' goods, but also to ensure that it can pay off its debts to Western banks.* This debt is current over $253 billion (owed to both public and private sources). Most of the incremental income from higher commodity prices would come right back to the industrialized world in the form of orders or interest.

The Northern hemisphere has still other reasons for moving in a more conciliatory direction. Let us note that while serious negotiations have taken place on the ten core commodities, these have been

---

*On the question of Third World debt and how it fits into the New (and the Old) Economic Order see Howard M. Wachtel; *The New Gnomes: Multinational Banks in the Third World,* Institute for Policy Studies, 1977.

limited to discussions of stockpiles of goods to be released in conjunction with market fluctuations, in order to maintain agreed floor and ceiling prices, and to the creation of a Common Fund to pay for the cost of handling such stocks.

UNCTAD had previously recommended that eight "other" commodities be included in the talks, but these seem now to have been lost in the shuffle and there is no calendar for putting them on the agenda. The "other" commodities are bananas, meat, vegetable oils, tropical timber, bauxite, iron ore, manganese and phosphates. Bananas and meat present special stockpiling problems; iron ore and phosphates are important only to a handful of developing countries (e.g. Liberia, Morocco). Their absence from the negotiating calendar can thus perhaps be justified for these reasons. But bauxite, tropical timber and vegetable oils—the last two especially important to a number of poor African countries—seem to have been somewhat arbitrarily abandoned. The immediate costs to the North of an NIEO would therefore very likely be limited to those relating only to the ten core commodities.

Even more serious for the UDCs, but reassuring for the rich nations, is the fact that there is at present no provision whatsoever made for discussing price *indexing*. This means that the "fairer and more stable prices" the UDCs might receive for their primary products are not linked in any way to those they will be expected to pay for imported industrial goods—which as everyone who has experienced Western inflation knows, are constantly on the increase.

The basic foodgrains, wheat and rice, also used to appear on UNCTAD's "shopping list" but are now omitted as well; in the crucial area of food which concerns us here, there is no indexing of, say, Egypt's cotton nor of Brazil's coffee to their massive wheat imports from the USA; no linking of Indonesia's rubber nor of Bangladesh's jute exports to the huge amounts of rice they must pay for in hard currency. It is, of course, the United States and to a lesser extent Canada, France, Australia and Argentina, that will profit from wheat purchases. More surprising to many people is the fact that the US outdistances both China and Thailand as the world's top exporter of rice. The lack of an index linking exported cash crops to imported food crops will constitute a continued threat to the economies of nations like Brazil, Peru, India, Egypt, Pakistan (heavy wheat importers) or Bangladesh, Sri Lanka, Malaysia, Senegal and Indonesia (dependent on imported rice). But it can only be of benefit to those industrialized countries which have special clout in the food trade.

In their bargaining stance, the "77" countries may be relying on stable prices for the major foodgrains they cannot do without and are not producing for themselves. If so, they are very much mistaken. In

8

the context of its heavy balance of payments deficits, the United States has an immediate interest in higher grain prices. Agricultural exports are indeed vital if the US is to avoid international bankruptcy.[7] As soon as wheat stocks in the US again approached glut levels and prices fell back from the 1973-74 highs, President Carter announced a 20% cutback in wheat acreage in order to reduce reserves and raise prices. Even more ominous noises come from a "Confidential Report to Executives" prepared by the Chase Economic Consulting Service, which examines the long term outlook (up to 1986) for the major American agricultural commodities.[8] It argues that standards of living in the developed countries will cause a continuing demand for more grain-fed meat and animal protein; that Russia should continue its policy of raising the dietary standards of its population and hence will continue to import cereals; and that population pressures in the UDCs will generate further demand. Not much can be done about raising price substantially between now and 1980, according to our friends at Chase, but from that date until 1986, prices should rise steadily until they again reach the record levels of 1973-74—i.e. about $4.50 a bushel for wheat.*

Chase does not discuss the forecasted prices for rice, but the US Department of Agriculture (USDA) has been steadily pursuing its market development programs for this grain, successfully competing with traditional suppliers like Burma, China and Thailand. Mid-Eastern and OPEC markets are growing especially fast. In early 1978, the USDA expected "continued strength" for rice prices and can be counted on to attempt to raise, or, at worst, to maintain them at present levels.[9]

Money Isn't Everything

Since America is one of the major customers for the core food commodities, UDC planners would be well advised to sit down for a few hours with US agricultural import statistics if they have not already done so. They would then discover that demand for what they have to offer is practically stagnant. The USDA classifies the nation's agricultural imports in two broad categories: "complementary" and "supplementary." "Complementary" foodstuffs are those products which cannot be grown in the US itself, like cocoa or coffee.

*An "International Wheat Agreement"does exist but it is toothless and more or less limited to exchanges of information. The 1971 agreement which was to end on June 30, 1978, has been extended for a year in hopes that further discussions between producers and consumers may bring about a stronger and more effective replacement. Chase, however, nowhere suggests that any international measures will affect prospects for US wheat prices one way or another. Barring a major breakthrough in brotherly international relations, this seems the more realistic approach.

9

"Supplementary" refers to products the US can raise, but of which it wants or needs more. This category includes meat, fruits, vegetables and oils. (It also includes sugar which is both a tropical and a temperate crop, but demand for sugar is steady as well so this does not fundamentally alter the reasoning that follows).

"Complementary" product imports reached saturation levels years ago, but there is ever-increasing demand in the US for such luxury "supplementary" items as fresh or frozen strawberries. If one takes 1967 as a base year with an index of 100, then demand for coffee, tea and cocoa has inched up to all of 103 in ten years' time. Compared to the same base year, sugar reached only 105 by 1976, while the index for *all* complementary products hit a puny 114 (and even this was mostly because rubber rose to 158 in 1976).[10] These "complementary" products are nothing but UNCTAD's core commodities under another name.

If we look at the same phenomenon from the standpoint of *value,* we find that during the two decades between the end of World War II and the mid-sixties, the US paid out a good deal more money for complementary than for supplementary products. Then the balance began to shift. Statistics for the seventies show a stable trend: during the seven calendar years from 1970 to 1976, the United States imported $20 billion worth of complementary (i.e. tropical, core products) but $40 billion worth of supplementary ones, or twice as much.[11] The US is moreover now buying substantially more of its supplementary national diet from UDCs than from other developed countries.[12] This means that the US is purchasing fewer and fewer core commodities proportionally to its total imports, but more and more food from the Third World. We will shortly examine why this is an important and a dangerous trend for the future of UDCs.

While it has become statistically evident that the Third World is progressively taking over the job of feeding already well-nourished Americans, while demand for its traditional products stagnates, the aggregate data we have just given cannot sufficiently highlight the situations individual producer countries may have to face. They must scramble (or kowtow) to keep the same customers from one year to the next. The same collection of USDA statistics illustrates this point: supplier countries can go from incomes of several million dollars to zero (or vice-versa) in a single year and have no guarantees as to the future intentions of their chief clients. Here is a sample of US imports of some core commodities; the fluctuations concern the changes that occurred between 1975 and 1976. The value of Brazil's sugar exports to the US drops from $100 million to zero. The Philippines, on the other hand, export over 800,000 lbs. of sugar to the US in 1975 and nearly three times that much in 1976. Guinea's cocoa exports to the US fall from nearly two million pounds to nothing and

10

Chad's from over five million to nothing; while Liberia and "other West Africa" make up part of the difference by jumping from zero to over four million pounds. Mexico's cotton exports to the US are halved, while India's increase by 400% and Pakistan's drop by 90%. For long fibre cotton, Egyptian exports are multiplied by four and Sudan's by fourteen but Israel's are reduced ninefold. Peruvian cotton exports meanwhile move up from zero to nearly eight million pounds.[13]

These examples are chosen among the more extreme cases, but they are meant to demonstrate the fact that major customers in the industrialized nations have an enormous choice of suppliers and that they are in a position to play one off against the other. Decisions in favor of some suppliers as against others may be made on political as well as on economic grounds.

Even assuming that prices are set at fairer floor/ceiling levels, no individual country is sure of selling uniform *quantities* year after year. This could make future national planning which relies on commodity revenues for replenishing the State budget just as problematical as it is today. Furthermore, it is far from sure that producer countries are fully aware of the flexibility of advanced capitalism and its adaptive capacity to the changing facts of economic life—and of trade. Substitutions for several core commodities that were unheard of ten years ago are now not only feasible but are being widely used. The case of jute is an obvious one—plastic bags and carpet backings make more durable and cheaper substitutes. Cotton has become almost a luxury fiber as synthetics have taken over greater and greater shares of developed country markets. Although everyone may know about plastic bags and polyester fibers, it might be revealing to take a poll of the economic planners in sugar-producing UDCs to find out how many appreciate the properties of high-fructose corn syrup; to learn in rubber producing countries how many persons in authority know about guayule; or in cocoa producing ones to what degree the plasticity of the soya bean is understood. Here are some of the more sophisticated steps agribusiness has taken lately.

When sugar prices skyrocketed in 1974, US agribusiness was quick to see the advantages of converting plentiful corn in to supersweet syrup. High sugar prices at that time caused so many companies to scurry into high fructose production that investment has resulted in some over-capacity, but as the *Wall Street Journal* remarks, "a very major segment of the food business may never be the same again."

Indeed, high fructose corn syrup is about twice as sweet as sugar and is especially well adapted to the industrial uses (soft drinks, jams, confectionery and bakery products) that absorb three-quarters of all

11

the sugar consumed in the U.S.* Consumer resistance to high sugar prices in 1974 also encouraged the syrup makers. US consumption of sugar hit a record 103 pounds per capita in 1973, but two years later had been curtailed to around 90 pounds. This was the result of a sort of blanket national refusal to pay the going prices for refined sugar and for products with a high sugar content. Meanwhile, per capita consumption of high fructose corn syrup is expected to double from 9 to about 18 pounds between now and 1980.[14] Add to this the fact that world sugar stocks have grown by several million tons every year for the past four years and now stand at about 27 million tons, or some 30% of annual world consumption—and one is left with an ideal context for continuing depressed prices.[15]

"Boom and bust cycles for primary products have occurred with such inexorable frequency and so exclusively to the detriment of the Third World countries that one wonders how they can still be taken in by the commodities shill-game."

How were tropical sugar-growing countries reacting while the industrialized nations were busily building high-fructose plants? They apparently took high prices in 1974 as a signal of shortages. Actually, sugar was even then fairly plentiful and high prices were largely the result of what I have referred to elsewhere as "planned scarcity." These countries nonetheless assumed that high prices were here to stay and immediately took the very decision guaranteed to wipe out any temporary shortage and to drive down prices: they planted larger and larger areas with sugar cane. Boom and bust cycles for primary products have occurred with such inexorable frequency and so exclusively to the detriment of Third World countries that one wonders how they can still be taken in by the commodities shill game. It is not entirely their fault. Because no mechanism for consultations among producers has been established (this smacks of "cartel" and is energetically discouraged by the North) they regularly and mutually insure their impending collective fate by rushing into world over-production like lemmings to the sea.

By late 1975, as was inevitable, the bottom dropped out of the sugar market and producer countries were left holding several million bags. An occasional supermarket in the US actually gave the stuff away—but so, literally, did the producers—because world pri-

---

*High fructose corn syrup recently received a kind of consecration when conservative Coca-Cola announced a switch from sugar to HFCS for one of its drinks.

ces at 10¢ a pound or less do not always compensate for the costs of production, even in low-wage countries. The new International Sugar Agreement provides for slightly higher prices, but it also imposes export quotas on participating producer countries. Since the US is the world's largest sugar importer, its decision to protect its own growers automatically affects outside suppliers unfavorably by reducing their commercial prospects. As if the common or garden laws of supply and demand (plus quotas) were not enough to face, Third World sugar producers have little cause for optimism in the short or long term: a brokerage firm quoted by the *Wall Street Journal* observes that while cost comparisons between high fructose corn syrup and sugar "are difficult to obtain, it is generally thought that corn priced at $3.00 a bushel is competitive with . . . raw sugar . . . at around six cents a pound." (In June 1978, corn was worth about $2.60 a bushel).

This economic data may seem rather dry, but what it means is that sugar exporting countries are placed in a no-win situation: If they increase sugar production, they create a glut and lower prices. They must, moreover, sell very close to cost if not below—otherwise they will encourage recourse to sugar substitutes. If they cut back production in the hopes of causing prices to rise, and if prices *do* rise, there will simply be even greater recourse to corn-based sweetners. Analysts of these phenomena note that once a substitute product has been adopted, the situation rarely returns to the *status quo ante*. Unless and until the price of corn used as raw material increases by at least 15%, there is no way poor countries can make a decent income on sugar unless they further squeeze their already low costs—which means cutting back on wages or on prices paid to individual producers. Demand could be further reduced. Even a country with a collective sweet-tooth like the USA has shown itself capable of reducing consumption by 13 pounds per head in a single year. Sugar is not, to say the least, a very sure bet for "export-led" economies in the Third World.

We may be telling a similar tale about rubber during the next ten years or so. Of course, synthetics have already cut into the natural rubber market for many uses; but the cost of petroleum (the basic ingredient in synthetic rubber) makes its use less attractive and radial tire technology requires natural rubber. This combination of circumstances has sent the price of natural rubber up to about 40¢ a pound and the major US tire builders are currently expanding their Third World plantations or improving the ones they have. So all is well for the rubber exporters? Not necessarily, for the companies have also rediscovered a desert shrub called guayule that grows wild in the Southwestern United States and that contains substantial quantities of latex.[16] It may take another ten years of R & D, but many people

13

> " ... even if producer countries obtain guaranteed and stable prices for their primary products, no law in the present or future world can promise them that they will be in a position to sell the same quantities as before."

are convinced that guayule will become a commercially viable substitute for natural rubber. Goodyear is already growing it experimentally and *Fortune* points out that guayule could have the added advantages of productively using marginal land while furnishing "potential employment for Indians." Widespread use of the shrub would also, of course, greatly reduce the current half billion dollar US import bill for natural rubber and consequently the revenues of producer countries like Indonesia, Malaysia, Thailand, Sri Lanka and Liberia. The tire companies want no part of an International Rubber Agreement that would increase prices paid to producers and if one were imposed on them "the rubber people in Akron are confident that if they are forced to they can devise new synthetics incorporating natural's remaining peculiar characteristics."[17]*

So we meet another double-bind situation for another core commodity. If the price goes too high, it will encourage synthetics and a crash program for guayule. Any "fair and stable" price in a future international agreement will most likely be set by the rubber industry which is in a better position to make the rules to suit its interests than are the producer countries.

But there's nothing like the taste of fresh roasted coffee or velvety chocolate, right? Wrong. Cargill has already invented a soybean-based chocolate substitute; while Su Crest prefers molasses as the raw material for its cocoa extender. Coffee substitutes may be based on anything from barley to oats to peanuts; all are quite capable of replacing 5% to 80% ground, roast or instant coffee depending on individual taste preferences, according to trade journals.[18] Consumer boycotts of high beverage prices only encourage further industrial experiments in substitutes.

What the foregoing discussion is meant to establish is that *even if* producer countries obtain guaranteed and stable prices for their primary products, no law in the present or future world can promise them that they will be in a position to sell the same *quantities* as before.

*Fortune does not mention Goodyear's two existing polyisoprene plants in Texas and Le Havre, France. Polyisoprene molecules are structurally identical to those of natural rubber. The only disadvantage to this artificial but truly natural rubber is its petroleum-based price.

America's acceptance of the 77's most pressing demands in this area would be an intelligent move on several counts: It would bring some economic gains to the US while Europe and Japan would pay the greater share of the costs; yet it would not prevent innovative capitalism from introducing alternative solutions exactly tailored to its own needs, thereby imposing a quota system for UDC exports in all but name.

Here an important qualifier is necessary. Although the West may agree to an Integrated Commodities Program and to a Common Fund for financing it, there is very little chance that it will accept any system that would effectively allow UDCs simply to produce as much as they like of core commodity X, Y or Z and sell it at a fixed price to a central authority. Here the opponents of these measures are quite right to affirm that no international agreement on earth could then prevent prices from sinking if unwanted stocks were allowed to accumulate yet still had to be financed. UNCTAD is aware of this and recommends "internationally agreed supply management measures, including export quotas, and production policies and, where appropriate, multilateral long-term supply and purchase commitments." It is also conscious of the substitution problem and hopes for "measures to encourage research and development on the problems of natural products competing with synthetics and consideration of the harmonization, where appropriate, of the production of synthetics and substitutes in developed countries with the supply of natural products produced in developing countries."[19] There is, however, no machinery proposed for allocating production among developing countries and it is hard to see how they are to be stopped from overproducing. It also seems utopian for UNCTAD to imagine, figuratively speaking, that high-fructose corn syrup producers like Archer Daniels Midland or CPC will one day sit down at the same table with the governments of Mauritius or Guyana to determine who has the right to produce how much of what kinds of sweeteners.

Perhaps the greatest advantage that industrialized countries, especially the US, would find in granting the minimum demands of the UDCs in this area is an ideological one. Such an attitude (whatever the very cold economic and political calculations behind it) would appear to the world as a generous gesture. The Third World would doubtless feel, for a time, euphoric until this victory showed its Pyrrhic face. How much time might then elapse between the implementation of all the *other* provisions that ought to make up a genuine NIEO is anybody's guess. The "77" would be told, in effect, that they were inordinately greedy after obtaining such startling concessions from the industrialized nations; that they should not ask for the moon. Except on a case-by-case basis, no debt relief would be forthcoming (and debts would still have to be paid back out of export

15

revenues). Agricultural processing, value-adding activities (although they, too, figure in the UNCTAD resolutions) would not be much furthered. Non-tariff barriers could well remain the same for the UDC's manufactured exports. Most important, no indexing of primary commodities to goods and foodgrains imported from the rich nations would have been introduced. Northern inflation would continue to be financed partially by the South.

Possibly the most alarming feature of locking oneself into the single strategy of the Integrated Commodities Program and the Common Fund would be the consecration of the present international division of labor assigning Third World producers the task of supplying certain raw materials (on other people's conditions) throughout eternity. Economic diversification could be retarded. Whole societies would be geared to supplying the needs of other, richer, people. By doing this, UDCs would continue to divert necessary labor from assuring food production, while remaining without any guarantee that the food they needed to import would be sold at affordable prices.

"One possibility of increasing UDC revenues that has been barely explored is that of increased trade between the Third World countries."

Is there any way that the drawbacks of this situation could be converted into plus signs? For, as we have noted, it is not morally or politically possible to come out *against* an NIEO for the Third World, however truncated. Outside of giving unrealistic and unwelcome advice to UDC negotiators to hold out for the perfect package, there are a few things that might be helpfully said. We, in the developed world, should try to make clear to any citizen of the poorer countries willing to listen that they should expect no presents from the USA in the way of food.[20] The era of relatively low grain prices in which we are currently living is not going to last if the US government and the US grain traders can help it. No national development plans involving wheat imports at under $3.00 a bushel should be made for the middle term—50% more than that remains realistic in the longer run.

One possibility for increasing UDC revenues that has been barely explored is that of increased trade *between* Third World countries. The whole emphasis of UNCTAD and most of the other international forums is placed on North to South, South to North flows. This is logical enough because these are the directions in which the trading patterns, the shipping routes, the banking and insurance

16

channels run and have run since the era of the colonial empires.

And it is true, of course, that intra-Third World trade is naturally restricted because so many UDC products are competing rather than complementary. Today, only about 6% of all world trade goes on between developing countries (only about 2.5% if oil is excluded). Surely with better communications among themselves, it should be possible to enhance inter-UDC commercial relations. These unnaturally low figures are themselves an argument for agricultural diversification—why not *food* trade as well between Southern hemisphere States? Such a strategy could be especially important for nations which, in a variety of ways, are attempting to make the transition to more equalitarian, democratic societies in the face of heavy odds. Mutually advantageous trade could turn out to be the most effective kind of international solidarity.

UDC negotiators could strengthen their position vis à vis the Center by making a concerted effort to buy all possible products from other UDCs before turning to Northern suppliers. They could furthermore, for many of their present imports, shift their purchases from industrialized countries whose opposition to the NIEO has been adamant (e.g. Germany) to those which have taken a more positive attitude (e.g. Holland, Scandinavia).

Such strategies will, however, be useless to the cause of true development if no overall social housecleaning and reordering of priorities takes place in the UDCs themselves. Assuming still that their NIEO strategy works, the *first priority* for use of any incremental income obtained through improved commodity prices *should be investment in agriculture for local food consumption*. Otherwise, there is every reason to fear that any gains from commodities will be literally eaten up by imports from nations producing the basic foodstuffs, and chief among them, from the USA.

However vital, such investment in agriculture will require a revolutionary change in the thinking of Third World nations that have until now conceived of "development" as industrialization at all costs. Government spending on agriculture—that is, on the sector where the vast majority of Third World people are active—is in most cases abysmally low. This state of affairs shows up clearly when summarized in the form of a table showing government choices as regards two categories of current expenditure: agriculture and defense. These figures may be usefully contrasted with those that indicate the percentage that the agricultural sector *contributes* to the Gross Domestic Product, i.e. to national wealth. Countries selected have all incurred serious food shortages in recent years.[21]

From these figures it is apparent that although farmers may contribute to their countries half or more of its GDP, they receive very little in return in the form of State services that could make their lives

COUNTRY	AGRICULTURE'S CONTRIBUTION TO GROSS DOMESTIC PRODUCT: % AVERAGE 1960-1973	AGRICULTURE AS % OF TOTAL CURRENT EXPENDITURE* (1973)	DEFENSE AS % OF TOTAL CURRENT EXPENDITURE (1973)
Afghanistan	54.2	1.4	24.3
Bangladesh	58	. . .	11
Brazil	18	2.1	13
Egypt	29.1	4.3	40
Ethiopia	57.8	2.8	19
India	49.6	3.4	27.7
Indonesia	46	. . .	26.3
Mali	46.7	5.2	18.9
Niger	52.3	7.	9.3 (1967)
Pakistan	38.5	2.8	51.7
Philippines	35	6.8	22.2
Senegal	34	5.6	11
Upper Volta	49	6.4	12.8

Source: World Bank, see note 21.

*"Agricultural expenditure comprises current expenditure for agriculture, forestry, fisheries, irrigation and land reform" (*World Tables* 1976, p. 12)

easier and more productive. Wealth they create is transferred into other pockets or provides new toys for generals. Investing in agriculture would not simply be more equitable, but more intelligent: when farmers' incomes rise as a result of greater productivity, their spending acts as a spur to the rest of the economy—not to mention providing it with far cheaper food than can be had via imports.

The reasons for some cases of bloated defense spending, such as Egypt's, are tragically obvious, but you may well ask who are the dangerous enemies of Senegal, Mali or Upper Volta whose governments all spend at least twice as much on defense as on agriculture. So many tons of paper and ink have been used to denounce the arms race that there is no way to avoid triteness when bringing it up. All one can do is point out that it is even more senseless in countries where a significant proportion of the population suffers from serious food deficits. "Defense" spending is now often used *to keep hungry, rebellious populations in check;* the hunger/arms equation is a self-perpetuating one.

We have already suggested, by noting the inequities of existing patterns of income distribution, that most of the increased revenues from commodities would accrue to the upper classes—perhaps one reason why UDC negotiators, also upper class, push so hard for them. But this is not a hard and fast rule. Whatever its limitations, the "trickle-down" theory does occasionally apply. Dr. Moises Behar of the World Health Organization notes, for example, that in Costa Rica there is a strong correlation between the world market price for coffee and the number of children hospitalized for malnutrition. When the coffee price is high, there is a lower incidence of disease and malnutrition and vice versa. Costa Rica is a country where coffee is largely grown by smallholders.[22] Peasant production is frequently the chief source of a great many of the core commodities. Most people are aware that cotton is an important crop for African farmers, but are surprised to learn that rubber, generally thought of as the plantation crop *par excellence,* is supplied to a considerable degree by peasants employing only family labor. In Malaysia, 55% of the whole rubber crop is collected in this way; in Thailand there are at least half a million small farmers that make this country the world's third largest rubber exporter.[23]

This is fine when, as in Thailand, the smallholders are primarily concerned with growing enough rice (or some other foodgrain) to feed their families, and devote themselves to the cash crop as a sideline without being dependent on it for physical survival. Such situations are not, unfortunately, the rule and cash crop price fluctuations can thus make or break smallholders. With stable and guaranteed prices, the small peasant would at least be in a better position to calculate the optimum use of his land and labor—*if* his own government

"Before the NIEO can do much good for anyone but the elites, economic justice must also obtain between the social classes in individual countries."

can be counted upon to pass on the cash crop revenues to him. For it is not enough that economic justice prevail between nations on a world scale. Before the NIEO can do much good for anyone but the elites, this justice must also obtain between the social classes in individual countries.

Business Week quotes, for example, US chocolate industry executives lamenting the fact that the policies of the Ghanian military government discourages farmers from producing cocoa. "'The farmer in Ghana gets about 16% of the export price of his beans and the military government gets the rest' groans the President (of the chocolate manufacturers). 'There's no incentive to produce'."[24] This may be bad for Hershey and Mars Bars, but it's worse for the Ghanian peasant.

There are two other strategies that mark a departure from the "trickle-down" ideology. They come under the catch-phrases of "Basic Needs" and "Self-Reliance"; often linked to "Collective Self-Reliance." Before looking at these important concepts, we should examine the kind of International Economic Order that is actually being introduced in the area of food and agriculture. Geared to feeding fewer and fewer people better and better it is being quietly introduced in the underdeveloped countries while their representatives are talking themselves hoarse in one international forum after another.

PART II

NIEO: The New Imperialist Economic Order?

I have tried to show some of the pitfalls of putting too much stress on cash crop, commercial commodities agriculture via UNCTAD negotiations and the like.[1] But there are other, more immediate dangers for Third World rural societies and they, too, originate in the wealthy, industrialized nations. Some of these dangers are already manifest; others will soon become so; all have to do with food *systems*. It is not an exaggeration to say that the economic, social and political futures of UDCs will largely be determined by the kinds of food systems they adopt.

Please note here the use of the term "food system" as opposed to "agriculture." Social scientists have got us all into the habit of thinking in terms of the Primary, Secondary and Tertiary sectors, supposedly embodying agriculture, industry and services respectively. Such a classification may have been useful sometime before World War II but it has relatively little to do with today's realities, especially in rich countries like the United States. In order to understand what is meant by a food system, one may imagine a line divided into three segments. The first segment is labeled "inputs," the second "food production" and the third "post-harvest;" or, if one prefers, "storage, processing and distribution." These three abstract categories apply to *every* human community (including those that don't farm—like Eskimos—if one replaces "harvest" with "catch") but their food systems will naturally vary enormously in length and complexity. The chain will be shortest in self-provisioning farming communities that rely on "natural" inputs (rain, self-reproduced seeds, hard work) and that store the resulting harvest on the spot. In shortline food systems, processing is limited to grinding and cooking—mostly breads and porridges; the producers and the consumers are the same people. The line is without doubt longest in the United States where industry has taken over the provision of all the agricultural inputs (including rain,

21

if one counts cloud-seeding); where the farming community itself is just a tiny segment of the line; where the storage, processing and distribution are immensely sophisticated operations and cost two-thirds of every dollar spent on food. Most academic research has focused on one or another of the divisions or subdivisions of the line (often on production alone) and has thus frequently not seen the forest for the trees.[2] Unless one tries to place particular aspects of food systems in their total context (not an easy job precisely because of the lack of research) one is likely to miss what is actually taking place. And what is actually taking place has, in my opinion, sinister implications for underdeveloped countries. I do not myself claim X-Ray vision, nor can I present an absolutely air-tight case in defense of this viewpoint; still there seem to me to be discernible and threatening trends in the evolution of Third World food systems which are worth close attention.[3]

Here are some hypotheses concerning food systems we shall be dealing with from now on:

(1). There is a recognizable pattern in the evolution of the food systems of capitalist countries; among them the US system is the one that has progressed furthest towards a high-technology type. This US system is tantamount to a *model* or paradigm towards which other countries are moving. This model will therefore, over time, tend to become unique.

(2). There is a concentrated effort on the part of the agents of the capitalist world system ("agents" in the non-conspiratorial sense of those who act, produce an effect); largely though not exclusively multinational corporations, to introduce the food system model they have devised at home to the underdeveloped nations. This is not being done with the aim of making UDC food systems independent and viable but rather in order to dominate them more effectively, so that the "periphery" may better serve the needs of the "center."

(3). This model has no relevance, past or present, to the needs and realities of Third World societies, since it evolved in the developed world under radically different circumstances. Indeed, it will be (and already is) enormously harmful to them, in particular because it perpetuates and reinforces hunger and malnutrition; still it is being accepted and put into practice with enthusiasm.

The fact that this model is both offered and accepted with such enthusiasm is doubtless due to the class interests, both in the industrialized and the Third World countries, that the model serves. These are real interests, and they are not playing games. I entertain, however, the naive hope that there may be cases in which this model is being allowed to penetrate rural societies in the Third World simply because no one authority there really understands what is going on. There may also be a remote chance of changing the perceptions of part of the "development Establishment"; one might, in time and with a lot of help, contribute to making certain approaches at least unfashionable. This could be important to the extent that Third World leaders may sometimes adopt development theories and "solutions" which they perceive as being fashionable in the West and which they erroneously equate with the notions of "agricultural progress" or "modernization."

Firms and Farms:
The US Food System

To understand the sort of food system that is gradually being introduced into Third World rural societies, we should first see how it operates in America as a prototype. Many American readers will know most of what follows concerning the US food system: they should either skip to page 32 or bear with the repetition of what may seem obvious. This study is not, however, addressed to an exclusively American audience and the rather detailed look at the high technology model and all it implies may be of some use as a "counter-example" to those who are searching for alternatives to Western-sponsored and Western-inspired development models. The US model *is*, unfortunately, relevant to what is now occurring in many UDCs; I am hopeful that the following pages will make this point clear.[4]

We will follow the same imaginary line, starting "upstream" from the farm itself at the inputs end. American farmers now spend over $85 billion a year on manufactured inputs and they are totally dependent on industry for every item that goes into food production. In former days (this is still true in some parts of Europe) "farms" were not vast stands of a single crop—they were complex operations involving both plants and animals—often several different kinds of both. In such polycultural operations, the farmer can be at least partially self-sufficient: seeds can be reproduced from crops (and exchanged with neighbors); animals provide much necessary fertilizer, pesticides are less necessary because the variety of plant species inhibits the spread of pests and disease; energy requirements may also be supplied on the spot when traction is provided by animals "fueled" with home-grown fodder.

All this changes with one or two-crop agriculture, and the changes have been particularly striking in the US in the past 40 years. For decades, American agriculture has been characterized by plentiful land and a shortage of labor, so productivity quite logically has been measured according to how much could be produced *per man*, not per unit of land. Under these conditions, farm machinery assumed enormous importance early on. Until shortly after World War II (when commercial fertilizers and pesticides also began to enjoy wide use) some especially expensive machines like threshers were jointly owned, thus spreading the costs of farm production among several cooperators. But this meant that the harvest had to be brought into the barn to await the arrival of the thresher—or risk spoiling in the field if bad weather struck. The shortage of labor to perform this extra task was such that cooperative ownership broke down and farmers came to prefer individual ownership of every machine, however expensive. This has become the rule since the late 1940s.[5]

In order to be able to buy industrial inputs and high-cost machinery, farmers must rely on credit from private banks (as well as on government loans). In 1977, outstanding farm credit shot beyond the $100 billion mark for the first time in history; it currently stands at about $120 billion and is expected to reach $225 billion by 1985.[6] Farm indebtedness has been heading skywards since 1973, a bumper year with exceptionally high farm prices. But as grain prices increased, so did the prices for inputs. Tractor costs, for example, traditionally follow grain prices up—but never down. So the massive expansion and equipment purchases undertaken on the strength of a very good year often had to be paid for subsequently out of lowered earnings. No expert denies that real farm incomes are declining and that the cost-price squeeze hits rural people especially hard. As one USDA spokesperson says, "Increases in debt have far outpaced increases in income . . . in terms of real purchasing power, a decline is expected (in 1978) . . . Difficulties will most often arrise with young operators who . . . have few financial reserves. Delinquencies among such borrowers are expected to rise."[7] This is a polite way of saying that a great many farmers are going to go broke and the hardest hit will be the youngest. They have not stopped going bankrupt, for that matter, since the middle 1930s when the peak number of 6.8 million US farms was reached. In the late 1970s, about 400 farms were dropping by the wayside every week. The total decline in forty years has been about 4 million farms; fewer than 2.8 million remain and the owner-operators of the top ten percent among them often buy up or lease the farms that fail. This is one factor that allows them, as a group, to take responsibility for two-thirds of total American agricultural production. These super-farmers are also the ones that profit most from public funds and according to *Business Week,* "practically all are millionaires . . . They are getting priority treatment by the banks while benefiting most from expanding government farm-support programs."[8] To make even greater economies of scale, to absorb all that machinery, all that new technology, the largest farmers are expanding at an unprecedented rate—at the expense of their smaller colleagues.

Large or small, they are more and more in the hands of their bankers who help them either to stay afloat or to expand. These bankers, like Continental Illinois of Chicago, one of the country's largest agricultural lenders, can be the owners of land rented or leased by farmers trying to make a start in the business or to expand their holdings. The Banks' terms for leasing land are stringent. Congressional hearings concerning a proposed mutual fund dealing in farmland disclosed that the terms of a typical lease ("developed by the University of Illinois [and] in wide use in the State of Illinois") leave the farmer scant freedom. It is the Bank, not the leasing farmer, who has the power to determine not only what crops shall be planted in what quantities, , varieties and sequence; but also what fertilizer is to be applied—the Bank can even decide to burn or to remove cornstalks and straw.[9] One witness at these hearings declared that "to protect (its) investment, the bank requires the farmer to plant crops the bank considers safe. In other words, if a farmer wants to raise hogs, the bank may say, 'Not with our money. You plant beans'."[10]

One of the reasons the farmer is so constantly dependent on outside sources of money is the burden of veritable monopolistic overcharges placed upon him by his suppliers. In 1972, the Federal Trade Commission found a lack of competition in the animal feed industry, dominated by Ralston Purina and Cargill. Such companies, according to the FTC, treated themselves to an extra $200 million in annual monopoly overcharges at the farmers' expense. The same observations held true for the farm machinery industry, still according to the FTC, except that here the overcharge amounted annually to a quarter of a billion dollars.[11] John Deere and International Harvester control 60% of the farm machinery market between them and thus can exert enormous leverage.

There is another aspect of the input end of the food system line which is not a tangible one but which still decisively orients American agriculture: research. Most of the research now carried out in this field in the US is done either directly by agribusiness companies or by universities working for them or for the USDA under contract. It is therefore not surprising that all their efforts are directed towards encouraging the kind of farming that will use optimum quantities of inputs; which will encourage higher and higher levels of technology (and, consequently, greater subservience to banks). The government also cooperates in reinforcing corporate control over agriculture through research: for example, when chicken processing workers claimed higher wages, the Agricultural Research Service of USDA helped out the processing firms by developing an efficient chicken cutting machine.[12] Pitifully little research is done on biological methods of crop protection or fertilizing; while a great deal is directed at greater use of chemicals. One example is the work on hybrid wheats which should drastically increase fertilizer use, or so this industry hopes.[13]

"Food processing and distribution are, for the most part, in the hands of oligopolies—a fact which few consumers understand because of the enormous, and purely illusory, diversity of labels gracing supermarket shelves."

What about those who occupy the middle segment of the line, the farmers themselves? Some of them are indeed millionaires (less than 300,000) in terms of land and equipment owned—but the vast majority makes less than $40,000 a year in *gross* sales. They also keep fewer and fewer of these dollars. Their problem is that their incomes are declining not only because of lower grain prices but also because costs steadily eat up higher percentages of their incomes. Before World War I, production expenses amounted to just half of gross farm income; in 1945 the farmer was still keeping about half of what he took in. Then began the rapid increase in costs—from $13 billion spent in 1945 by over 5,800,000 farmers to $85 billion spent in 1977 by fewer than 2,800,000. Inflation? Partly—but the *proportion* of costs in relation to income has increased during the same period from 50% to 80%.[14] Hung with mortgages and the need to buy ever-more sophisticated equipment to remain competitive, dogged by uncertain prices; it is no wonder that so few young people can make a go of it in farming. The average investment *per worker* (including the owner-operator) in agriculture is now more than $400,000, or approximately ten times the amount it takes to create a job in industry. The average age of the US farmer is 50.[15] A small farmer who started out in the late 1940s and who had his mortgage all paid by 1960 may have survived to the present day—but those who entered farming later are today often in difficulty. For those who are determined to remain on the land, the only way to fight declining family incomes is to expand the land base.[16] Three articles of the iron law are more land, more machinery and minimum paid labor—preferably just family work-force. It is this system that turns the farmer into a *homo lupus homini,* but not all can survive the competition. As a member of the Canadian National Farmer's Union put it to me, "The pursuit of self-interest eventually becomes the pursuit of self-destruction." The farmers' segment of our line is shortest of all and represents less than 4% of the total US population.

What of the segment "downstream" from the farm—that is everything that happens to food between the farmer and us, the consumers? This is the longest portion of the line, the one that represents the most added value (i.e. cost); it is also the one that agribusiness is attempting every day to make even longer! Food processing and distribution are, for the most part, in the hands of oligopolies—a fact which few consumers understand because of the enormous, and purely illusory, diversity of labels gracing supermarket shelves. A company like Beatrice Foods (number 36 on *Fortune's* latest "500" list) with annual sales of over $5 billion, markets 8,000 different products and has bought up over 400 companies in the past twenty-five years.[17] The top fifty food processing companies make about three-quarters of all the profits in the industry. Figures for 38 leading companies show profits an average of 10% higher in 1977 than in 1976, with many well-known companies (Hershey, Hormel, Nabisco, Pillsbury, etc.) chalking up profits jumps of 20% or more.[18]

Agribusiness spends less on research and development than virtually any other industry in the US, and what they do spend is geared to reducing their costs and to increasing their share of consumer purchases—not to better food and nutritional value. Nutritionists have every reason to be alarmed about the amount of ersatz put in our food, but they do not, perhaps understandably, examine this question from the company's point of view. The company knows very well that ersatz is economically indispensable if one wants to operate nation-wide. Additives can insure long shelf life and apparent freshness; chemicals do not fluctuate in price like honest-to-goodness food and can thus be subjected to accurate cost-accounting; ersatz is flexible in the lab and lends itself equally to soups or sauces, puddings or pies.[19] The food business is one where costs are relatively low, technology relatively uncomplicated and rewards unusually high for the services (?) rendered to the consumer.

"Agribusiness spends less on research and development than virtually any other industry in the US, and what they do spend is geared to reducing their costs and to increasing their share of consumer purchases—not to better food and nutritional value."

Economists generally agree that if 55% or more of a given market is controlled by four or fewer companies, then an oligopoly exists. This is the case for *every* major food category in the United States. In milling, the top four firms hold 75% of the market; for bakery products the figure is 65%; fluid milk 60% and milk products 70%; processed meat 56%, bananas 85% and all canned goods 80%. For canned soups, Campbell's alone controls about 90% of the market.[20]

The breakfast food industry also wins a ribbon for concentration, with four companies holding over 90% of the market. Describing current Federal Trade Commission litigation against these companies, in an article unreservedly favorable to the latter, *Fortune* explains that:

> The evidence . . . shows an industry that is bitterly competitive in every respect but price. Hundreds of thousands of dollars are invested to develop a product that will have unique 'mouth feel'. . . When we're beating each other's brains out every other way, the cereal companies have said in effect, why compete on price, which consumers say isn't that important?[21]

Which consumers say price isn't that important? Is this what "consumers would say" if they understood how much they are being bilked by the food industry, not just for breakfast foods but for virtually everything else they eat? Americans are now spending over $150 billion annually on retail food purchases. No one knows how much of this outlay is unnecessary and due solely to oligopolistic pricing practices.

Vertical Integration

One of the biggest changes in the food industry since World War II has been the drive toward vertical integration. This term simply means that individual companies attempt to control as many segments of the line we have been describing as they possibly can. Some buy up seed companies (Cargill, Anderson Clayton, General Foods); or institutional feeding operations (Del Monte) or supermarkets (Weston Group of Canada) or chains of restaurants (Ralston Purina, Pillsbury, Heublein, etc.). You can integrate backwards towards inputs or forwards towards the final consumer, but there seems at present to be no single corporate policy towards agricultural production itself in agribusiness strategies. The food industry's relationship to farming itself has been a stormy one. Many companies began "corporate farming" in the 1960s, but a few years later most had decided that it was preferable to let real farmers take the risks of inclement weather and blights. Although there are some spectacular new corporate farming ventures like Boeing's potato growing operation in the Pacific Northwest (that's where McDonald's french fries start life) the far stronger trend seems to be towards contract farming. By 1970, more than half of the total US production of foodstuffs was already taking place under vertical integration (the company runs the farm itself) or under production contract (the company signs up farmers and tells them what to do). Highest integration is in vegetables for processing (95%), fresh-market vegetables (51%), citrus fruits (85%), potatoes (70%), fluid milk (98%), broilers (97%), seed-crops (80%) and sugar (100%). The crops still being sold on the open market in overwhelming proportions were food and feed grains, cotton, tobacco, oilseed crops and livestock (excluding chickens).[22] Whereas in 1970, about 22% of the entire US food supply was produced through vertical integration or under contract to a food firm, this figure was expected to reach 50% by 1980 and 75% in 1985.[23] In other words, this food is being grown either by hired labor or by farmers working under stringent corporate specifications. Should these laborers and farmers attempt to organize and demand higher wages, prices or better working conditions, the company has the option of closing down and moving elsewhere, as Del Monte, for example, has done. The farmer has nowhere else to go; his one advantage over the laborer (who has only his two hands and relative mobility) is that he still owns his land. But how important is this factor in a country where, as Jim Hightower has remarked, the question is not so much who owns the farm as who owns the farmer?

This is, then, a very brief outline of the US industrial food system model. Given a choice of three words to describe it, I would choose: Waste, Concentration and . . . . Efficiency.

This food system is wasteful.[24] Nearly everyone is now aware that huge amounts of grain are fed to livestock and that animals are quite inefficient converters of grain into meat. Animals therefore entail waste (unless pasture or scrap-fed), but it is characteristic of sophisticated food systems to transform cheap calories into expensive ones because most people find expensive calories (e.g. meat) more pleasant to consume. It is also well known that agriculture in the developed countries frequently absorbs more energy in the form of fuel and inputs of all kinds than it gives back in calories—but again this is to be expected where there is a market for greenhouse lettuces and the like.[25]

Most experts concede that *no country on earth,* including the US, has yet reached the outer limits of the meat and dairy products its citizens are capable of consuming if they have the money to do it. Agribusiness, of course, encourages such indulgence and feedlot animal raisers are going into the meat packing business as well, just to make sure they keep hold of both ends of this profitable stick. Further waste is incurred in the proliferation of processed food. For readily understandable reasons of their own, the corporations are not interested in selling us items in bulk that have undergone little processing and which cannot command a highly profitable price. The companies' goal is to add to the *cost* of food, but not to its real *value,* however much economists may speak of "value added" in the transformation process. The more steps a company can add to the line that separates the final consumer from the farm gate, the happier it will be. This is why Americans are perhaps the only people on earth privileged to buy unbreakable, perfectly calibrated, dehydrated, rehydrated parabolic potato chips packed in vacuum-sealed tennis ball cans—at dozens of times the cost of the original, long-forgotten potato. The US food system is geared, in its entirety, to getting people to eat money.

This food system is concentrated. We have already given some figures on the oligopolies that exist both upstream and downstream from the farm. Whatever one's opinion of free enterprise and the virtues of competition, the American food system does not exemplify them. Oligopoly control does not only mean the possibility of keeping prices to consumers higher than they would be under circumstances of true competition—it also means that a miracle is required before any other company can enter the field. The companies already there have their access to banks and to raw material suppliers sewn up—they also have the huge cashflows necessary for maintaining the barrage of advertising messages to consumers. In fact, the only people who can get into an oligopoly are other oligopolies—like ITT into bakery products and seeds or Greyhound busses into processed meats. Such newcomers are unlikely to rock such a comfortable, high-powered and profitable boat.

"Americans are perhaps the only people on earth privileged to buy unbreakable perfectly calibrated, dehydrated, rehydrated parabolic potato chips packed in vacuum-sealed tennis ball cans—at dozens of times the cost of the original, long-forgotten potato."

Exceptionally high concentration is already a fact both upstream and downstream from the farm, that is, for inputs and processed food products. It also looms as a clear and present danger for hundreds of thousands of farm families who have little chance of survival. The USDA Office of Planning and Evaluation in 1975 prepared for Congressional use a document detailing three possible futures for American agriculture.[26]

What comes across clearly in this study, based on computer simulations, is that barring a crash program to encourage and save the smaller farmers, the farm sector is going to shrink drastically. Even if

" .... some 300,000 family farms will disappear by 1985."

such radical action is taken, some 300,000 family farms will disappear by 1985. If approximately the same government policies and interventions that obtained between 1930-1970 prevail, 600,000 fewer farmers will be on the scene in 1985. If, however, the scenario of the "Maximum Efficiency Future" is adopted—and this means mostly not consciously adopted, for it is enough to do nothing at all and let nature and capitalism take their course—then "market forces" alone will allocate resources and the strong will devour the weak. This is perhaps the most likely of the three possible scenarios; its major features have, in fact, been incorporated in US agricultural policies since the late 1960s. If "Maximum Efficiency" is what is wanted, then seven years from now 1,680,000 farms will have failed—or 62% of the present total! *All* of the million remaining farms will be selling over $40,000 worth of produce each year, and yields will have improved, thanks to intensive technology, by 89% over the end of the 60s.[27] Of course, as the USDA explains, "the consolidation of uneconomical small farms into fewer and larger farms capable of fully using new technology and minimum cost production will require that some farm people choose off-farm employment."[28] This "choice" is, *mutatis mutandis,* comparable to the "choice" exercised by consumers over food prices; it will necessarily increase the numbers of rural and urban unemployed.

This food system is also efficient. You might feel that a food system is efficient if it assures every member of the national community of a decent, sufficiently varied and nutritious diet at a reasonable cost. On such grounds, the US system does not measure up very well since over 12% of the population is now living below the poverty line and several million Americans are unable to eat decently because of lack of purchasing power. Junk food sales have increased appallingly as availability of fresh produce has declined. Working class and especially minority families pay high prices for processed foods with little nutritional value.[29] But no one with any clout measures "efficiency" in terms of usefulness to people's health and livelihood. The criterion of efficiency for the US economy in general and for the food system in particular is merely how much profit it generates. The more profit, the more efficient the system. Certainly there is nothing very complex about this notion economically—one may indeed consider such terms of reference extremely crude at a time when even the World

Bank is beginning to use what it calls "social indicators" to measure the efficient performance of national or regional systems.

Agribusiness Goes Abroad

What have these observations concerning the US food system to do with food systems in the Third World and with a New International Economic Order? More than meets the eye: the companies that have been largely responsible for entrenching the control of this system in the United States are not national but *multi*national and the model they have devised for the US—efficiency and all—is being proposed, or imposed, in UDCs.

What is wrong with the previous chapter? Among possible criticisms is this one: The description you have just read assumes, for the sake of clarity, that the American system exists in a vacuum "made in USA." As just set forth, it would appear to be self-contained, nothing enters it from outside food systems and it is apparently without influence abroad. Nothing could be farther from reality.

There are any number of links between the food systems of the "center" (the rich industrialized countries—the US being generally seen as the center of the center) and the "periphery" of poor, underdeveloped nations. The first link that usually comes to mind is the one originally forged by colonialism which we have already examined from the particular angle of the NIEO in Part I—the export of primary products and agricultural raw materials from the periphery to the center. Less well know, perhaps, are the exports of what the USDA calls supplementary products; in this case fruits, vegetables, fish, meat and flowers that flow from South to North in response to growing market demand in the rich countries. We will be coming back to both kinds of cash crops.

But what of flows in the other direction—from North to South? An attempt to analyze them requires that we imagine another line representing another, more labor-intensive type of agriculture employed in Third World food systems. It is obvious that food is actually produced and consumed in the poorer countries under an enormous variety of social and economic conditions—this line is thus not meant to be a picture of any society in particular, merely to illustrate some of the more common characteristics of Third World food systems. Upstream, on the input end, we find low levels of capitalization and few manufactured inputs. Research, when it is carried out at all, is frequently restricted to cash crops, although international research institutes have done work of a very particular kind on food grains. Credit to the agricultural sector as a whole is usually niggardly; legitimate bank loans naturally go to the best commercial risks and usury takes over from there.

The central segment representing agriculture *per se* is far longer than the corresponding segment in the US, since half or more of Third World populations is generally rural and tries to find a livelihood in farming. The proportion may be under 50% in areas of Latin America but can go as high as 95% in parts of Africa. Downstream, processing can be limited to the threshing floor and the family kitchen in a completely self-provisioning food system or it may involve sales of surplus by peasants to a local or regional market or to a State board. The State, or private enterprise, may also manage centralized storage and processing plants in the major cities. But even here, the level of capitalization is generally low. This, in any case, is a very schematic description of what Third World food systems *used* to be like. They are currently undergoing rapid change because, on the one hand, exploitation of cheap UDC land and labor for cash crop production has increased ever since perishable yet air-freightable crops have been added to the list of export commodities; on the other hand, every segment of their food chains is being modified by influences from the North. Perhaps the easiest way to test this proposition is to place the two imaginary lines one above the other and examine what the vertical relationships are between them. (See the appendix for a graphic summary of some of these relationships). This will give us a kind of simple model which has two uses: it can first summarize the nature and extent of Northern penetration of Third World food systems. More important, it can provide a tool for *predicting* what the following stages of this penetration may be. If it is true that the ultimate tendency of the capitalist center is to create a single global food model—but one in which UDCs will remain subservient to the dictates and needs of the center—then it is important that we have an idea of the roads capital's initiatives are likely to take.

A few short remarks on the suggested model. First, it is not intended to be quantitative, although other people might want to find out just how much has been invested in fertilizers, post-harvest technology or what-have-you in country X or continent Y. This would be useful work, but quantification necessarily implies something that is over and done with—it cannot be more than a photograph of a situation at a particular moment and cannot account for the dynamic, forward movement that is leading us towards a single, integrated world food system.

Second, it will be quite impossible to comment here on all the interconnections and implications contained in the model. I merely hope that other researchers may find it useful for situating their own work in a more general context. Third, there is a basic ambiguity in the use of this model, because it seems to picture exactly what the Western world usually understands by "development." "Underdevelopment," in turn, is conceived of as a lack, an absence of elements that can only be supplied by the center—in the present case, the various elements of the high-technology food system model. Needless to say, this is not what I understand by development. The model is meant to be descriptive and possibly predictive, but in no way prescriptive—it does not suggest a direction that *ought* to be followed, quite the contrary. Nor, conversely, does it imply that past or present food systems in the UDCs, unsullied by foreign intervention, are models of equity. Refusal of Western "development" goals does not mean that one need defend usury, exploitation of peasants by landlords and the like.

Finally, while the model should be seen as dynamic and open-ended, as a kind of mirror of an on-going process, it is also important to understand that the phenomena that can be fit into it are spatially and temporally interdependent. For a Third World rural society, it is almost as hard to accept one part of the model and simultaneously to oppose all the others as it is to be, as the old joke goes, "a little bit pregnant."

The pace and rhythm of the changes introduced may be quite different according to the part of the model involved. The Center may find that it has almost no trouble imposing its presence or introducing its methods in one sector but that it meets with strong resistance in another. The trend, however, will be towards integration of the entire UDC food system into the larger whole.

Logic tells us that the same causes will produce the same effects. What, then, are the foreseeable results of imposing upon radically different societies a food system that grew up under social conditions peculiar to the United States? It is reasonable to say that as agriculture becomes an entirely mercantile operation in Third World countries, a great many small peasants who do not have the wherewithal to become capitalist farmers will have to "choose" irregular wage labor or migration to the cities in hopes of a problematic job, just as their counterparts have had to do in the US. The difference, of course, is that industrialized societies have relatively more jobs to offer them. More and more standard and luxury produce that can be grown cheaply in the periphery will take up the space, time and effort that should be devoted to food crops—for while the food systems of the UDCs are to become "like" the central one, this does not mean that they will be any less dominated. The Center will dictate the division of labor and will be the prime beneficiary of the "vacuum cleaner effect" that sucks the agricultural wealth of the periphery northwards. Small businesses and local processing efforts will fail as multinationals enter the field. MNCs are financially able to wait as long as necessary for this to happen. Storage and processing will become more centralized with good results for agribusiness but unfortunate ones for self-provisioning communities. More and more food will be fed directly to animals. But we are getting ahead of ourselves . . .

Naturally, it is impossible to explain everything with a single hypothesis. Nonetheless, and whatever its drawbacks, this schema is the only method I have yet discovered for imposing some sort of order on thousands of events and rapidly shifting reality. The empirical evidence seems to fit. I think the basic intuition—that a gradual takeover of Third World food systems to suit the needs of the center is occurring—is fundamentally correct.

If so, this means that ultimately—and, of course, figuratively—when the super-system has at last been realized, diversity will be dead. We shall then have the Global Factory for producing standardized seeds and inputs. They will be financed by the Planetary Bank and used on a normalized farm by a plastic peasant. The commodities grown will be given universal processing in order that they may be sold in the World Supermarket to consumers who can pay a price set by agribusiness. Millions of people will be unable to participate in this system and, at best, will survive on its fringes if they survive at all. Too pessimistic, too apocalyptic for your taste? Let us hope you are right. Let us hope also that those in a position to stop the long march towards food-system uniformity may act before it is too late.

Agribusiness Upstream from the Third World Farm

Multinationals are the chief agents of penetration of Third World food systems, but they are frequently dependent on the prior efforts of center governments or of the international development agencies for providing infrastructure and employable personnel. The World Bank and the several UN specialized agencies have been instrumental in creating many of these indispensable underpinnings of industry—like electricity and adequate transportation—while agencies like USAID have concentrated on training personnel that will be receptive to a particular sort of food system. Between 1950 and 1969,

35

USAID trained 43,000 foreigners in agricultural sciences in the United States; this figure does not include all those persons trained abroad by Americans in the field.[30]

The major foundations also play an important role. Foundations are in a unique position because they are accountable to no constituency (except a hand-picked board). Unlike corporations, they are under no pressure to obtain immediately profitable results and can thus indulge in long-term planning. Authorities of the underdeveloped countries in which they operate generally perceive them as being at best benevolent, at worst neutral; but rarely as adjuncts of American commercial or political policy. Foundations may thus have access to persons and places the government and the corporations cannot reach. This was certainly true of the Rockefeller and Ford Foundations in India during the early 1950s when State relations were cool. Or, as the Vice President of the Rockefeller Foundation explained to a Congressional committee, The International Rice Research Institute in the Philippines (funded by Ford and Rockefeller, an architect of the Green Revolution in Asia) "because its scientists are independent" has access to countries as impenetrable as Burma.[31]

If the package of new agricultural techniques that together make up an unfamiliar agricultural model are to be transferred successfully, there must be agents willing to undertake the unprofitable aspects and wait out the initial acceptance period so that the companies need lose no time when they arrive upon the scene. The President of the (Rockefeller-funded) Agricultural Development Council put it this way:

> There is a tendency to give the credit for a breakthrough to the *last essential element to be added* (to an agricultural system, his emphasis). And if you look, for example, at the places in the world where within the last four years the Green Revolution has made extensive and even extraordinary progress, they are those parts of the world and those parts of individual countries where prior to that time the other essentials of agricultural development were already in place.[32]

Green Revolution is the catch-all phrase for the "modernized" agriculture that the center is touting in the periphery. Since I have dealt with this question elsewhere,* I prefer to stress here less well known aspects of the package. Seeds furnish one very good example of the trend towards uniformity.

Year after year, these sources of our future food crops are being mercilessly wiped out as agribusiness gains more and more control

---

*How the Other Half Dies, Chapter 5.

over seeds. Whereas even a few years ago thousands of local varieties of food grain plants still existed in the so-called 'Vavilov centers' of genetic diversity,

> Suddenly in the 1970s, we are discovering Mexican farmers planting hybrid corn seeds from a midwestern seed firm, Tibetan farmers planting barley from a Scandinavian plant breeding station and Turkish farmers planting wheat from the Mexican wheat program. Each of these classic areas of crop-specific diversity is rapidly becoming an area of seed uniformity.[33]

The seed companies are sowing ecological disaster as they reduce the world's genetic base. When farmers decide to stop saving seed and start buying it on the market, their families then eat the whole of the previous year's crop: "Quite literally the genetic heritage of a millenium in a particular valley can disappear in a single bowl of porridge."[34]

The two chief characteristics of hybrid seeds are that they are particularly are prone to blight and disease and that they cannot be self-reproduced. Plant breeders (and pesticide manufacturers) are only a jump or two ahead of the pests and diseases that thrive on the new "prey" as one biologist calls these crops that have not had time to adapt to natural predators and to dangers in their environments. Only reinforced chemical treatments can protect them ... so no one will be surprised to learn that in the past few years family-founded seed companies have been bought up by such chemical firms as Sandoz, Ciba-Geigy, Purex, Pfizer and Upjohn. Investments in seed companies are attractive in themselves, aside from any side effects on chemical sales. Sales inside the US have boomed, increasing by about 20% annually for the past several years, and gross margins for these companies are commonly 50% or more. US seed company sales abroad went up "only" 38% in the first three years of this decade: "Foreign markets are opening slowly but they are extremely attractive," says one executive. Another comments, "This is one hell of a profitable business."[35]

It is not necessarily the farmer's fault if he buys the kinds of seeds that require plenty of chemicals. For one thing, hybrids, if grown under proper conditions, give higher yields to the acre, so he often prefers them even if it means he must repurchase new seed every season and use greater quantities of other inputs. For another, the processing company to which he may be under contract will insist on seed X or Y because it wants a uniform product. This naturally also reduces the choices available to consumers. Fruits and vegetables are genetically selected for characteristics valuable to agribusiness—such as adaptability to mechanical harvesting—not to nutritional content or just plain taste.

Industry is pushing hard for universal legislation that would protect new genetic types with what amount to patents. One industry spokesman explains that a UDC has "the simple option of a huge investment in plant breeding research and testing for its own environmental conditions, or the passing of legislation under which the private international plant breeder can carry out this work."[36] The word "international" and the fact that the gentleman making this recommendation works for a major chemical corporation lead one to conclude that this "private" plant breeder is not some unknown geneticist experimenting in his lonely laboratory, but is, rather, an employee of a multinational firm which hopes to gain even greater control over seed use through legal measures.

Profit-making enterprises cannot indulge in the long term view; thus the companies do not appear alarmed that genetic disaster—like the nineteenth century Irish potato blight and famine, but on a twentieth century scale—may be just around the corner. Perhaps our one white hope to avoid such induced catastrophe will be found among the poorer "backward" peasants the development planners so often accuse of being "resistant to modernization." A Swiss anthropologist has told me of his field work in an Indonesian village which had, like many other villages under official pressures, adopted the hybrid rice seeds of the Green Revolution. They stuck it out for two harvests but they disliked the taste of the new rice; what is more, they were convinced it was less acceptable as an offering to their deities. So they returned to growing their traditional varieties. I asked him how it was they still had these varieties to fall back on. It was, he said, because they had continued to set small plots aside for growing the eight or ten different varieties required for ritual offerings. To those who see this as a typical example of mystical or "pre-logical" behavior, I would reply that it also shows an enormous amount of ecological and agricultural scientific wisdom however deeply buried in religious custom—for many communities after two harvests of hybrid rice would have had no traditional seeds left at all.

Green Revolution seeds will only grow with fertilizers, controlled irrigation and drainage, and chemical protection. That the multinationals have an important stake in providing these inputs is obvious; that this connection was early recognized and fostered by their friends and allies is explained by a Mr. Kreisberg, who has links with the USDA, USAID and the Ford Foundation: "The agricultural modernization (the new seeds) signal could be the seedbed of new market economies in the world's low income countries," he says. One of the "implicit objectives" of US foreign policy is to encourage systems in UDCs in which "private enterprise plays a larger role . . .". The new commercial agriculture will aid this aim because it is "rooted in modern technology." Green Revolution farmers must "make eco-

38

nomic ties to a wide array of agribusinesses—manufacturers of agricultural equipment and chemicals, storage and warehouse operations, processing firms and distributing organizations . . . Businessmen from the more developed economies and international lending agencies are all engaged in efforts to increase fertilizer capacity, improve water supply and spread the use of the new technology."[37]

While the Green Revolution has created any number of commercial opportunities for the sale of seeds, diverse agricultural chemicals, irrigation equipment and the like, they do not *necessarily* demand mechanized cultivation. Farm machinery has proliferated in the Third World not so much because it is economically justified as because of a desire on the part of the wealthier, larger farmers to do away with the administrative and social problems presented by hired labor—especially hired labor which is quick to notice the higher Green Revolution yields and to draw the relevant conclusions concerning fair wage scales. US multinationals have helped to confirm such landowners in their belief that machinery can greatly reduce the level of social unpleasantness they must bear. Here is one instance:

> The year was 1968, the setting a large, level wheatfield in the state of Punjab in Northern India. Nearly 10,000 farmers and many government officials were gathered to watch two John Deere self-propelled combines . . . demonstrate the practicality of mechanical harvesting in India.
> The spectators, most of whom had never seen a combine before, lined the edge of the field as the two machines cut wide swaths through the waving grain. At the end of each hour, the two combines . . . were stopped and the work they had done was calculated and announced . . . (The) figures were quite incredible to the farmers, because it usually takes three to four men an entire day to cut one acre of wheat by hand . . . The results of this and several other John Deere field days held in India prompted the government-owned Punjab Agro-Industries Corporation to import 60 Deere combines and offer to harvest wheat and rice for farmers on a custom basis. The custom harvesting service caught on fast and eventually spread to other irrigated areas. Today, hundreds of self-propelled combines are being used in the most productive wheat growing regions of India . . . The combines also eliminate the dependence on large numbers of farm workers at harvest time.[38]

Various Asian authors note that low-interest government loans have helped larger farmers to mechanize, which they see mostly as a means to "get rid of tenants and to keep for themselves whatever portion of the harvest (a third to a half) used to fall due to the tenants. Mechanization primarily reduces the need for labor at all stages of cultivation and does not increase yields substantially." In fact, "costs involved in mechanization are higher than the corresponding profits:

if purely economic criteria are applied, pumps and irrigation equipment are far better investments than machinery."[39]

The situation is similar in Latin America, where it is estimated that two and a half million jobs were lost from the time of the first large-scale use of machinery up to 1972.[40] In spite of this heavy use of machinery (and of a lot more fertilizer), "average yields of a large number of farm products have improved very little, particularly if compared to yields in other parts of the world and, in certain cases, within the same region." The governments of South America also collaborate with the richer farmers to make it virtually impossible for landless laborers to find employment; indeed, getting rid of labor is:

> usually rational at the level of the individual farm. These management decisions are made within the context of import subsidies for modern farming machinery and other inputs, over-valued exchange rates, low or negative interest rates and special tax concessions to encourage mechanization. Labor troubles, payroll taxes and increasing social unrest in the countryside provide further incentives to reduce the labor force.[41]

The consequences of this high-technology farming accompanied by greatly reduced employment opportunities have been higher food prices, highly concentrated land holdings, reduction in real wages for those lucky enough to have work, and rural migration which merely displaces poverty from the countryside into the cities. Large-scale mechanization might have made sense in the wide-open spaces of the US where few extra hands were available for farm work, but contributes to social disaster in Asian or Latin American circumstances.

"The consequences of this high-technology farming accompanied by greatly reduced employment opportunities have been higher food prices, highly concentrated land holding, reduction in real wages for those lucky enough to have work, and rural migration which merely displaces poverty from the countryside into cities."

With the onset of the Green Revolution, purchased inputs become the rule, just as they did in the US, and farmers grow increasingly dependent on outside financing. "The necessary *mercantility* of the new technology elevates the credit-worthiness of the producer into an asset of the highest importance, on a par with skill in husbandry."[42] At the same time that firms profit from input sales, banks expand by providing credit to this entirely new market. Usually, only the farmers with connections and collateral are considered for credit, but there are signs that Western banks may at last have noticed the small farmer. If the model we are following is of any use, it should encourage us to take such signs seriously, even though present penetration of this sector by outside interests is embryonic. Consider the speech delivered by Professor Michael Lipton of the Institute of Development Studies, Sussex, to an audience of professional bankers. The following excerpts are as summarized by the FAO Bankers Programme; (emphasis or parentheses are mine).

> Professor Lipton's theme was the neglect of the small farm sector by commercial agribusiness and credit systems in developing countries, and the need to correct this situation through a new approach by banking to the problem of rural lending. Small farmers . . . though they disliked risk, were efficient in their use of resources, responsive to price changes and swift to innovate; (they work hard) and hence obtain more output per acre . . . And yet emphasis is almost always on large units . . . . rural organization is biased in favor of large farmers while agribusiness is geared to bulk supplying of large units. But one important part of the explanation (for this bias in favor of large farmers) lies in the rural credit system. There were two extreme views about agricultural finance and rural credit. One view is that small farmers are inherently non-credit-worthy. This was demonstrably untrue—default/loan ratios were higher for large farms than for small. The other view is that good projects would attract credit anyway. This applied to only a very small proportion . . . The banking system could play a major part in improving this situation, but only by abandoning much of its 'conventional wisdom': by *lending at higher interest rates to the small farmer* and insisting on repayment, but, on the other hand, by being ready to meet his consumer as well as producer needs and to accept *unconventional forms of security* (wives and daughters?) At present, lack of adequate and timely credit was preventing many small risk-prone farmers in developing countries from obtaining steady, modest rises in income and output from the new cereal technologies. Efficient organization to improve this was a major challenge to the world's banking system.[43]

At least one bank may have heeded Professor Lipton's plea: "Barclay's International announced its willingness to provide funding for the first phase of a programme to establish the current needs for training materials in agricultural credit in developing countries." Barclays would undertake this as a follow-up to the recommendation of the FAO World Agricultural Credit Conference that "much more emphasis (should be placed) on the training of credit field staff in developing countries."[44] One reason small farmers have had such a hard time obtaining credit is that banks view administrative costs on loans of "insignificant" sums as prohibitive. But if private commercial banks can train enough low-cost personnel to overcome this difficulty, we soon may see Barclays Barefoot Bankers tramping throughout the Third World countryside.

For it would be logical that capital's next move be towards the integration of smaller farmers into the mercantile structures of market economies; towards the extension of the Green Revolution to those who have not yet been able to adopt it. This cannot be done without credit, and if the provision of such credit turns out to be profitable for Western banks, they will not hesitate to broaden their horizons.

It is all the more important to chart agribusiness' and banking's next moves in UDCs when we recall that a mere fifteen years ago, the Green Revolution scarcely existed in the field (except in Mexico). But once the welcoming committee—the foundations, USAID, *et al.*—had its work done, the number of hectares planted to the new seeds literally exploded. In less than ten years, the area grew from about 50,000 hectares to more than 32 million and is still climbing. Pakistan, for example, imported 50 tons of the new seeds in 1966-67 and *42,000 tons* the very next year.[45]

Lately, there has been so much criticism of the social effects of the Green Revolution that many people largely responsible for it have crawled back into the woodwork and are lying low. Others, like Lester Brown, no longer claim that the Revolution has caused world hunger to disappear, but insist that it has "bought us time."[46] Time for what? Neo-Malthusians like Brown would answer that it has held off starvation "while we search for an answer to the population problem." Other observers would say that the time bought was paid too dear in the currency of millions of peasants' ruined livelihoods and that the damage is irreversible. Consider the case of India, as described in a confidential report prepared for the World Bank. What has occurred during this bought time that has proceeded with Western blessings? The number of agricultural laborers in the Indian workforce increased, between 1961-71, by 20 million, or more than 20%. Lester Brown might be quick to point out that this in itself reflects runaway population growth. How, then, would he explain that the number of cultivators *decreased* from 93 to 78 million during these same ten years? It is also significant that the number of *women* cultivators dropped during the same period from 27 to 9 million. The deteriorating status of women is partly caused by "growing indebtedness which leads to loss of land." Women must then become farm laborers if they can find jobs: 5 million did manage to be hired during this ten year period, increasing the number of female laborers from 10 to 15 million, but their position in the *total* agricultural workforce is in constant decline. The Bank also cites "sale of land by marginal farmers and outright eviction of sharecroppers . . . There has been a renewed concentration of landholdings, agrarian reform

42

nonwithstanding . . . (in one district) 95% of the farmers held only half the land; 5% owned the balance. This is not exceptional."[47]

The Asian Development Bank (AsDB), another of the chief promoters of the Green Revolution, also remarks on what, in buying time, we have actually purchased: greater hunger and unemployment. Its report covering thirteen Asian countries over the past decade concludes that agrarian reform has been a failure, that absolute numbers of malnourished people have increased, that real agricultural wages have declined and that already catastrophic unemployment figures have been exacerbated by Green Revolution technology. The worst-off countries—India, Indonesia and the Philippines—are precisely the ones where "modernization" of agriculture has made the greatest progress. For the AsDB, "the region is no closer to solving the food problem than ten years ago."[48]

There is an important question one should ask at this point—a question for which I have no clear-cut answer. Have Western interests concluded that the growth of commercial agriculture in the poor countries is faltering because the social classes that can practice it are severely limited in numbers? Should they seek a new stratum of "beneficiaries?" Surely they have recognized that the innumerable peasants forced off the land by high-technology farming are not finding jobs in mushrooming cities, nor indeed anywhere else. The World Bank, for one, while not actually pronouncing the fateful words "Green Revolution," is presently talking about extending the techniques it entails to the small farm sector. We have seen that the commercial banks may also have a nascent interest in providing the credit that would allow poorer cultivators to get themselves locked into mercantile, "modernized" farming. If the hypothesis of a universal food system is valid, then it would seem that the next step may be to introduce elements of it into the self-provisioning sector which, though deeply scarred by the social effects of the Green Revolution, has as yet been unable to contribute to the profits its generates. "Small farmers" are coming into vogue inside the development "Establishment." This is all to the good if it means helping them to hold onto their land, to produce more food *for themselves and their immediate communities,* to escape the clutches of landlords and moneylenders. To date, however, such altruistic aims have not intruded noticeably on the plans of capitalist transformation of Third World societies.

A more likely scenario is, perhaps, that "small farmers" will be introduced to the joys of agriculture geared not to feeding people but to making money. They will aid the expansion of input suppliers; to pay for their purchases and to reimburse their loans, they will sell their harvests immediately, sometimes to other agribusinesses. If the ruling rural bourgeoisie that has already adopted the Green Revolu-

43

tion attempts to impede its extension farther down the social ladder, it could even happen that Western "development" planners decide to sacrifice segments of those classes that have proved themselves altogether too greedy, in order to preserve the major features of the system as a whole. Power-watchers would do well to keep an eye out for this tendency, for one unfailing and frankly admirable characteristic of capitalism is its enormous adaptability.

The Green Revolution was originally conceived not only as a way of expanding US agricultural inputs markets but also as a means of (1) obtaining adequate food supplies for the urban masses (2) creating a stable, prosperous rural bourgeoisie in the UDCs—in a word, of insuring social control without agrarian reform. Its advocates doubtless did not foresee the full implications of what Andrew Pearse has called "the talents effect"[49]: in the Green Revolution as in the Gospel, "to him that hath shall be given; and from him that hath not shall be taken even that which he hath." As rural unrest increases, ways to placate less favored small farmers will have to be devised. Extension of the Green Revolution to them—if necessary at the expense of part of the landholding elites—may well be one of the strategies chosen.

Wiring the Third World Farm Into One World Market

The whole point of an integrated world food system is that one produces not for human need but for "the market." In "the market," whether national or international, if you don't pay, you don't play. Companies who can find paying customers orient demand, and if demand runs to strawberries in February, strawberries will be grown regardless of the pressing food needs of millions of powerless and penniless people. Food systems, even in UDCs, are also fashioned to transform primary, cheap calories (like those eaten in the form of cereals) into more profitable calories (like those found in meat and processed foods).

The Overseas Private Investment Corporation (OPIC) is the US government agency that specializes in "political risk" insurance and equity loans to US firms setting up shop in the UDCs. As of the end of 1977, its roster at least 45 "active" projects concerned with ranching or animal raising in poor countries (there are in addition a great many other projects of this kind considered "paid off"). Industrial chicken raising ventures and beef cattle ranches are especially popular activities for OPIC's loans and insurance.[50]

While Third World chickens may sometimes eat food suitable for humans, more often their feed is grown on land previously devoted to food crops; in both cases they are niggardly in returning protein consumed, as only about 25% is retained. They are, however, excellent converters of *value* and especially good customers for processed feeds. Robert Ledogar, in a book which deserves to be widely read,[51] describes how Ralston Purina simultaneously sets up feed mills and a chicken industry so that its feed will find a ready market. What goes into the feed mill? In one case, soya and sorghum. Ledogar reports that in one valley in Colombia, before Ralston Purina moved in, sorghum acreage stood at zero and is now over 60,000 acres. Soybeans, which previously covered about 15,000 acres rose to over 140,000. Neither crop is suitable for direct consumption by people. The company's operations have been extremely well-managed: from 1966-71, annual broiler production doubled to 22 million birds; egg production doubled between 1970-73 to two billion, while Ralston Purina in 1973 sold 240,000 tons of feed in Colombia. A remarkably efficient system, except that "for about a quarter of the population, a dozen eggs and a kilogram of chicken cost the equivalent of a weeks' earnings or more." The overall protein deficit in Colombia has grown since the company arrived.

The President of Purina's international operations has a somewhat different perspective and explains that

> If we can identify national development objectives and can contribute to them as good corporate citizens, then we will move in in a small way in agribusiness. As these nations develop, we will branch out into other things that we do and which the economy needs . . . We bring more efficient agricultural technology to the farmers who supply us with grain inputs and to the livestock producers who use our feeds . . . For example, in Colombia, when we went in, we found a shortage of carbohydrate raw materials. There wasn't enough to divert from direct human consumption into livestock. We brought in agronomists and grain sorghum seed . . . We offered farmers a guaranteed price for the grain.[52]

Whether or not there was "enough to divert from direct human consumption," human consumption has suffered. Not only can poor people not buy chicken and eggs, but in this same valley the acreage now devoted to feed crops has caused cultivation of dry beans to decline drastically: there are now about 42,000 fewer acres devoted to this staple of the ordinary Colombian's diet than before the arrival of Ralston Purina.

While this particular product goes to middle and upper middle class consumers in Colombia, a lot of the protein that originates in the UDCs heads due North. This is the case for almost all the beef cattle raised on Central American or African ranches and it is also the case for fishing ventures, another favorite area for foreign investment in Third World food systems.

The Latin American Agribusiness Development Corporation (LAAD) whose only stockholders are fifteen or so multinationals like Ralston Purina, Castle & Cooke, Cargill, etc. has invested in a number of projects that concern chicken, hog or beef raising and processing. LAAD explains that:

> the world food crisis has dramatized the need to increase food production in the developing countries . . . Of the world's developing areas, Latin America offers one of the best potentials to increase food production. Fortunately, most Latin American governments are giving higher priority to food production and rural development than in the past.[53]

From this, one can only conclude that the "world food crisis" has hit North America especially hard, because that is where the produce grown by LAAD-financed companies invariably goes. The Corporation has also perfected a fool-proof profit making system. First it obtains loans of several million dollars from USAID (that is, from American taxpayers); these loans are long term and carry interest charges of 3-4%. LAAD then reloans the money for agribusiness projects in Central America (adding capital of its own) and is paid back in the short or medium term at "interest not in excess of 9% per annum."[54] LAAD's avowed interest is in "non-traditional" export crops which "include beef and beef products, fresh and processed fruits and vegetables; cut flowers, dried flowers, ferns and tropical plant cuttings, semi-processed and finished wood products, seafood and other specialty items." Guatemala is host to the largest number of LAAD projects followed by other Central American countries, but the consortium is also branching out into South America and the Caribbean.

Prior to 1950, practically all the fish eaten in the North was also caught in northern waters. Today, between a third and a half comes from UDC's seaspace. Very little of this commercial catch serves the needs of populations in the southern hemisphere countries. Of the whole Peruvian anchovy catch, 80-90% is exported as fishmeal to provide feed for industrially raised chickens. Many people hoped that aquaculture or "fish-farming" would help to solve food shortages in poorer countries and it is true that in China carp ponds are an important part of village economies. Unfortunately, experts point out that aquaculture requires precise and delicate control over the reproductive and growth cycles and that the species that lend themselves best to existing technologies happen to be those, like shrimp, whose price is prohibitive for all but the best-off consumers.[55] Such delicacies will never help feed hungry people. Nevertheless, as the international market for fish expands, more and more projects of this type are being set up in the Third World, including at least thirteen insured by OPIC.

Ghana is one of the several African countries to have been hard hit by food shortages in 1977-78.[56] Thus OPIC assistance to Star-Kist (owned by Heinz) for a tuna venture there is of particular interest. Here again, when we read successive OPIC Annual Reports, we are led to believe that "shortages" especially afflict the rich countries:

> What few people recognize is that the growing demand for tuna fish and other seafoods in the United States and elsewhere has placed a strain on available supplies. Thus Star-Kist has embarked on an international program which can help to alleviate future shortages. (1974).

Star-Kist has organized an effective international division of labor for this fishing venture: A large loan from OPIC allowed it to purchase US fishing vessels equipped with the latest Japanese technology:

> Currently the daily catch is unloaded at the company's modern refrigeration plant in Tema (Ghana) and then shipped to Puerto Rico for processing and eventual sale in the United States where tuna has been in limited supply. (1975)

"In the agribusiness international economic order there is every reason that American cats take precedence over West African people, since the former can pay and the latter frequently cannot."

This was phase one. Phase two of this project has now been completed. An existing Ghanian mackerel cannery (mackerel is a very cheap fish) has been converted to tuna processing. It is fulfilling the expectations of Star-Kist, since it has an:

> annual capacity for producing 206,000 cartons of canned tuna and 67,000 cartons of tuna cat food. (1977)

In the agribusiness international economic order there is every reason that American cats take precedence over West African people, since the former can pay and the latter frequently cannot. The population of the US now stands at 212 million people, but the number of *consumers* is closer to 277 million, because one must take into account the 30 million cats and 35 million dogs who eat over $2 billion worth of processed food annually. Cheaply produced meats and fish from the UDCs make up a good bit of their menus; dog and cat food are also among the most profitable items agribusiness has to sell and are therefore aggressively promoted.[57]

You Take the Risks, We'll Take the Profits

The old economic order involved plantations and the kind of domination in which a company receiving a concession assumed all the rights (though rarely the duties) of a totalitarian State over its territory. One account of companies like Lever Bros. (now Unilever) in the Belgian Congo makes this quite clear:

> The system of large Leopoldian concessions and of forced labor ... brought about an enormous historical leap in the Congo. Mercilessly crushing the old African agrarian system, the finance companies proceeded to make gigantic expropriations, seizing millions of hectares, burning villages, tracking down the population far from the rivers, displacing and deporting them, forcing them to gather plantation crops at gunpoint.[58]

Clearly, things can no longer be done this way. As the opportunity for such brutal exploitation has waned with changing political conditions, the companies have adjusted their methods and are prepared to adjust them further. Many are still producing the tradiitional cash crops found on the UNCTAD list, but they are not necessarily doing it with land that belongs to them. In our time, they indeed prefer not to be encumbered with land, and even the huge traditional agribusiness kingpins like United Fruit (now United Brands) and Unilever are ridding themselves of unwanted property. One obvious reason for this is the danger of nationalization, but there are other and more subtle business necessities contributing to this changed *modus operandi*. In Part I we discussed the possibilities of substitutions for the major cash crops of which the developed world is taking full advantage. These considerations also affect the policies of MNCs in the Third World. We may take the example of Unilever, the world's largest importer of fats and edible oils (probably 50-70% of all the imports in the world). Unilever's consistent strategy is to be able to manufacture its soaps and margarines with whatever oil is most advantageous at a given moment. This is not only technically feasible—it is economically vital, for one should never be caught short by price fluctuations on the world market. Here is what a former Chairman of the company says on this point:

> The aim is always to enable us to switch from one oil or fat to another without any loss of quality ... (the various attributes of the products) must not be impaired ... Subject to that imperative, we are trying at all times to put ourselves in a position to use less of the oils

and fats which are in short supply and more of those which are easier to get . . . Our research has, therefore, been directed for years to making us more flexible, more able to use as many different oils and fats as possible for as many purposes as possible.[59]

In these circumstances, Unilever has no reason to lumber itself with African plantations which may—even with very cheap labor— at times produce costlier goods than can be had elsewhere. One exellent candidate for such replacements is soya oil from the US which used to be a primary product but which is now sometimes difficult to get rid of as the by-product of a vastly expanded animal feed industry. One student of the subject even concluded that

> The evolution of the edible fats and oils markets is moving towards the gradual elimination of tropical oils inherited from colonial days, since these are now in competition with products that give a good yield of meal along with low-priced oils as by-products.[60]

Multinationals should, above all, be flexible and ownership is not conducive to this aim. There are other ways of controlling land without tying one's assets down. One business school professor put it succinctly: "The leasing boom . . . has rendered obsolete the once prevalent ownership ethic [in Third World countries]."[61]

This of course does not mean that the companies no longer control both production and marketing of traditional cash crops. They are merely learning to shift the risks attendant upon agricultural production from their own shoulders to those of the host country and— more important—those of its farmers. Nestle has become the world's second largest food corporation without ever owning a single cow or a single acre of coffee or cocoa bushes.[62] It prefers to let a local farmer own them, care for them, and pay for them, frequently thanks to a loan from Nestle, while assuming the more profitable activities for itself.

Here we may return to OPIC for an illustration of the modern approach to cash crop farming. OPIC has supplied equity capital and lent over half a million dollars to "Tea Importers Inc." for a project in one of the poorest African countries—Rwanda, where annual per capita income is $65. The project is to include a tea-processing factory, so it may bring in some needed foreign exchange. But who is to furnish tea to the factory?

> The typical Rwandan farmer owns an acre of land or less and raises crops primarily in order to feed his own family. The project will enable some 2,500 such subsistence farmers to sell tea as a 'cash crop' and roughly half the population in the region surrounding the factory is expected to derive sales income and to benefit from the project's profit sharing plan.[63]

49

Any farmer with an acre or less of land is already having a hard time feeding his family year-round. If he uses it henceforward for growing tea, he will have no food source at all and will become dependent for his entire livelihood on the international tea market (Unilever-Lipton, Brooke-Bond Leibig, etc.). If there are profits to share, so much the better—but if there are blights, poor harvests or low world prices, then these 2,500 farmers and their families may very well starve.

In spite of the often-verified fact that cash crops are not secure sources of income, many governments are now branching out into production for export of "non-traditional" crops like those favored by LAAD. This can prove to be an even more dangerous course to pursue than the cultivation of coffee or sugar, because, unless quick-frozen, all of these new-style products are perishable. Research done to date on such ventures shows enormous profligacy in the use of resources, all of which are devoted to providing luxury items for consumption in the wealthy countries.

In spite of vast domestic production, the US has become the world's largest importer of beef. Firms responding to a hunger for "meat of modest quality at prices much lower than those of American sellers" find it in Central America. Before 1960, ranching in these countries was entirely devoted to satisfying local demand, but during the decade from 1962-72, beef *production* increased only 5% a year while beef *exports* went up at least 18% annually (and have gone higher since). Since populations are also larger, the net result has been that many Central Americans have had to give up eating meat. Under normal circumstances, ranching is carried out on land good only for pasture. But in Central America, the largest latifundia owners are the ranchers, and they raise cattle on land that could perfectly well serve for food crops:

> Extensive cattle raising does not take place according to the theoretical rules of optimum allocation of resources; the structure of land ownership forbids this ... Herds are not found just on the least fertile land or in the most under-equipped areas—far from it ... Cattle raising has shored up the latifundia system. Ranching occupies half the arable land and uses 5 million hectares to produce what could in fact be produced on half or a third that much. It is a usurper of land and has contributed significantly to the defense of huge estates.[64]

Ranching for export (pet-food, fast food for people) wastes land resources and ignores the food needs of local people. New-look fruit and vegetable projects are similar in their impact. Perhaps the best proof is to be found in a book written by Professor Ray Goldberg of the Harvard Business School to extol and encourage projects of this kind.[65] Goldberg, in the wake of Professor John Davis at Harvard, practically invented the concept of agribusiness and was one of the first, if not *the* first, to apply a systems approach to agriculture. While I personally feel that he directs his skills (and his students) towards absolutely wrong priorities, there is no faulting his thoroughness nor his talent and what he writes should be taken seriously because it is taken seriously by the US and foreign governments. His analyses of several cases of fruit and vegetable production in Central America are thus most revealing, and what they show is an alarming waste. It goes without saying that none of these products is intended for local consumption since export production for North American winter markets in exchange for hard currency is the goal. The word "nutrition" surfaces occasionally in the studies, but it always turns out to be the nutrition of American consumers between December and March that is involved. In contrast, the producing countries have a *real* nutrition problem; the *average* daily calorie intake is 1,930 calories in El Salvador, 2,130 in Guatemala, 2,140 in Honduras, etc.; of course the poorest people in these countries eat even less.

But leaving aside the question of export crops versus local consumption and taking these projects on their own terms, the losses of food at every stage are enormous. If the crop survives drought or maladies or poor cultivation techniques in the field, it may still rot in a packing shed or on its way to the port or in the ship that takes it to Pompano Beach. If by some miracle it arrives intact in Florida, it can still be refused because the fruits and vegetables are too small or the wrong color or simply because the broker already has enough okra or melons or whatever to sell that day. For a book that contains a great many arithmetical and statistical tables, it is a pity that these losses are nowhere added up; still it is a fairly easy task to determine that for the stages of picking and packing *alone,* "rejects" of melons in Honduras amounted to 81%, for cucumbers in Guatemala 82% and for melons in El Salvador 90%![66] Production costs were frequently much higher than revenues and US brokers (whom the Central American producers all consider dishonest) sometimes refused up to a third of all deliveries. Brokers only accept the produce "on consignment" when they accept it at all; this means that the producer bears the risk of spoilage or failure to sell right through to the final purchaser. Under these circumstances, producers are lucky to recoup their costs, much less make a profit.

Even "rejects" did not go to local people, although in some cases they were a source of animal feed. Goldberg explains that one of the priorities of the projects is to provide employment; however, in the case of Guatemala, 70% of the cucumber pickers are children under 15. The "sorting and grading for export was done by 27 women who were paid $0.80 per day . . ."[67] One large grower has solved the labor problem to his satisfaction:

51

> In order to motivate his workers in the packing stations, Sr. X has ranked them according to three categories, with different pay scales. A worker can be moved up or down at any time, depending on his work and the judgment of Sr. X.[68]

Señor X received free technical assistance from USAID, as did the Callejas Bros. of Nicaragua. The latter are not what might be termed "small farmers," since they invested several hundred thousand dollars in their vegetable operation and employ 440 people in menial occupations as well as eight managers. USAID did not choose to give technical assistance to any of the cooperatives or smaller farmers who lost the most money on fruit or vegetable exports, but it did help to get the ball rolling generally by co-sponsoring a seminar on air-freighting with Pan American Airways.[69]

In spite of huge losses of both food and capital, despite the obvious malnutrition of large numbers of local people and working conditions which would, one hopes, shock Professor Goldberg if they obtained in his own country, there is no criticism in this book (written under contract with USAID) on any of these points. The whole approach is that these projects are fundamentally beneficial and need only to have the "bugs" worked out by employing a proper "systems" approach. The countries concerned will have to invest in infrastructures and transportation networks, import better inputs, and especially devote their "educational delivery systems" (sic) to training people at every level to understand the agribusiness approach.

> In effect, the educational delivery system, like the commodity system, must be market oriented. Educators (should) provide the participants not only with skills to carry out their responsibilities more effectively, but also with a vision of the new society into which they have been recruited.[70]

Perhaps it is not necessary to point out that the market orientation is that of the US market and that this new society is being determined for Central Americans by foreigners.

Ernst Feder's study on Mexican strawberry production for export[71] is valuable not only for the empirical evidence it presents of waste (the soil is literally mined), dependency (all the inputs come from the US); but also because he offers the useful reminder that smaller agribusiness corporations are just as important—if not more so—as the giant MNCs everyone talks about. Their scope is geogra-

phically and financially more limited, but their transactions are he
same, and taken together sometimes more important than those of
the huge food firms.

"Every time American farm workers gain a victory, they are handing agribusiness an invitation to seek its land and labor beyond US borders."

Strawberries are a relatively recent addition to the Mexican agricultural scene, whereas fruit and vegetable production for export has been going on in the Mexican State of Sinaloa for half a century. Here the similarites with American agriculture are striking, as is the degree of incorporation into the US food system. The farms themselves are enormous: 85 landlords control 117,000 hectares, and these same families oversee input distribution, local commerce and banking. The level of technology is as high or higher than in the US and investments of $2,000 to the hectare of tomatoes are not unusual. Tractors, airplanes, laboratories, agricultural chemicals—all the inputs are American, except for the labor. Since Mexico now has an estimated 7.5 million migrant workers (many of them *permanent* migrants) the growers have no trouble hiring at low wages (migrants' wives and children come even cheaper and are much appreciated); even so they are increasing mechanization and by 1970 used machinery on 65% of the land. The number of landless workers in Sinaloa doubled between 1960-1970. However powerful the landholders may be *locally,* they could do little without their American partners who, once again, are not the major MNCs but smaller agribusinesses, specialized wholesalers and distributors.[72] Sinaloa thus serves (1) as a major market for US-manufactured farm inputs and (2) as a permanent supplier of year-round labor intensive crops to US markets.

Every time American farm workers gain a victory, they are handing agribusiness an invitation to seek its land and labor beyond US borders. Capital is mobile, whereas labor is mobile only when it suits the needs of capital (as in the case of migrant workers). Even if North American demand for these fruits and vegetables is uneven, this is of little consequence because foreign investors have very little capital tied up in growing operations and no obligations whatsoever towards their workers. Profits may fluctuate from one season to the next, but they do not disappear. Poor countries, on the other hand, assume the risks of climate, disease and poor sales; they also are increasingly willing to orient their *whole societies,* not just their farming sector, towards the provision of luxury crops to Northern markets a few months of the year. Goldberg's analyses show that it is not just a question of using scarce land and inputs for exports rather than food crops, but of changing infrastructures, transport, communications and even education to suit the needs of export crop systems. One must credit Goldberg with recognizing early on that for food systems to become *agribusiness* systems, all the different elements should be supplied at the same time, and not on a piecemeal basis. Over ten years ago, he saw that the US businessman in the Third World had an opportunity to apply "his know-how and the *total market concept* (his emphasis) to the requirements of various food systems of other nations"... (There is a need for an) "integrated approach to ... developing food economies which recognizes that all parts of the agribusiness system—farm supplies and operations, food processing and distribution—must fit together."[73]

Although Goldberg's advice has not been taken to the letter—no agribusiness consortium has yet managed to take over a Third World food system in one fell swoop—in another few years his goal may be nonetheless accomplished. Fifteen years ago, the Green Revolution was still largely a gleam in the Foundations' eye. Not every sector can be as effectively nor as rapidly penetrated by Western capital as the input end of the food system, but all are moving in that direction.

We should not assume, however, that the Sinaloa model of huge farms and wealthy landowners ready to keep migrant labor in line for the benefit of US partners will be the only model for servicing the world food system. There are signs indicating that agribusiness will try to preserve and to use smaller peasants because they are willing to supply *their own and their family's labor for almost nothing.* This will be especially true for the peasant who has enough land for self-provisioning and who can raise a cash crop on the land left over: *whatever* he makes for the cash crop, it is still, so to speak, money in the bank. There is no problem for modern management in dealing with a large number of peasants prepared to work extremely hard for a small return—far harder than plantation laborers with no stake in their yield. The company always retains the option of refusing produce not of 'export quality' and maintains at all times its superior bargaining position. This is why agribusiness increasingly favors the "satellite system" of contracting with many local farmers.

This trend on the part of food firms will also reinforce the embryonic trend in banking previously mentioned: provision of credit to smaller peasants allowing them to purchase the necessary inputs; although in some cases the agribusiness may assume the banker's role itself.

Agribusiness Downstream From the Third World Farm: Anything They Can Do We Can Do Better

When we looked at the US food system we saw that the part of the chain between the farm gate and the consumer is the one where the most value is added and the most money made. Space even for a short history of the multinationalization of US national food firms that has taken them from Canada to Europe to the UDCs is lacking here but is not necessary since it has been well done by others.[74]

People interested in the current geographical distribution of agribusiness may refer to *Who Owns Whom* or other standard company directories. The UN Center on Transnational Corporations is also doing valuable work on food processing firms set up in the Third World and has established a classification system for situating their activities. A company may begin with sales in a UDC of processed foods manufactured elsewhere and imported; it may then move on to the procesing in UDCs of imported raw materials. The "mature" stage will involve processing of the host country's own raw materials for local sale but especially for export.

Brazil and Mexico are invariably the first targets US agribusiness picks in the Southern hemisphere because of proximity to Northern markets, the existence of prosperous middle and upper classes able to compete with consumers in the rich countries and a long tradition of warm welcome for US capital. After Latin America, US MNCs generally proceed to Asia and, much later, to Africa—the continent with the least multinational investment. European and Japanese food firms tend to head first for their former colonial areas.

As noted in the last chapter, the trend is toward the 'satellite' project in which local farmers furnish the agricultural raw materials to a central shipping or processing point. They may be supplying fresh, airfreightable produce (e.g. the House of Bud in Senegal); traditional cash crops (Gulf & Western sugar operations in the Dominican Republic; the tea-growing Rwandans); or non-traditional cash crops (LAAD-sponsored vegetable or beef processing projects in Central America). Depending upon the affluence or the poverty of the local market, greater or lesser parts of the satellite-processed produce will remain on the spot or be disposed of on the world market.

Here I prefer to concentrate on aspects of the chain "downstream" that are perhaps less well known; readers are again referred to my book and to other sources listed in the notes for examples of agribusiness processing activities. The essential point has already been made—money is the magnet that draws food. Either land once devoted to cheap staple food for people is converted into land producing animal feed crops, or local farmers are induced to grow not for local consumption or even for self-provisioning, but for the national or international market. Food becomes nothing but merchandise, and the surprising thing is not that so many people are undernourished but that farming still actually feeds as many people as it does. From present trends, it seems fair to state that agriculture will continue to feed a minority of people better and better with more expensive calories and that concomitantly more and more nonparticipants in the system will go hungry.

New Weapons in the Grain Arsenal

Henry Kissinger made a long speech at the World Food Conference; it bears re-reading nearly four years later. Two things he mentioned which largely escaped notice at the time were these:

> (1) We also plan a number of new projects. Next year (1975), our space, agriculture and weather agencies will test advanced satellite techniques for surveying and forecasting important food crops. We will begin in North America and then broaden the project to other parts of the world.
> (2) . . . There is no substitute for additional investment in chronic food-deficit countries. (Some of the several investments needs can be) financed locally. But substantial outside resources will be needed for some time to come. The United States believes that investment should be concentrated in strategic areas . . . (one) major priority must be to reduce losses from inadequate storage, transport and pest control. Tragically, as much as 15% of a country's food production is often lost *after* harvesting because of pests that attack grains in substandard storage facilities.

Kissinger touches here on two matters we will discuss in turn: the US "early warning system" via earth satellites and the food-saving strategy now designated by the term "Post-Harvest Technology." Up to now we have concentrated on everything that is sucked *into* the US food system from the underdeveloped world and have scarcely mentioned the importance of grain exports to the US economy. Agricultural exports now earn over $26 billion annually for the United States and keep its trade balance deficit from being even worse than it is. Staying ahead of the competition in this area requires copious and faultless information and the satellite program Kissinger spoke of is part of the vital information gathering network. Earth satellites make an inventory of the entire planet every nine days and they are the basic instruments for the Large Area Crop Inventory

56

Experiment (LACIE) sponsored jointly by the USDA, NASA, and the National Oceanic and Atmospheric Administration (NOAA). Beneath these layers of acronyms lies a powerful new tool serving American domination of world grain markets. "USDA's goals in LACIE are to develop and test a system for predicting foreign crop production through the use of advanced satellites and computer technology together with current and historical weather and agricultural data." This is not quoted from a critic but from the official year-end report on LACIE to the USDA steering group.[75] The program started off gradually, doing inventories of wheat on the Great Plains which could be ground-checked for accuracy. Since these results were judged satisfactory, the program was next extended to Canada and the Soviet Union and is now overflying and analyzing the wheat crops of China, the USSR, India, Brazil, Australia, Argentina, Canada and of course the USA. The seven other countries are all major clients or competitors of the US for wheat sales. Canada has agreed to be overflown and exchanges information with the USDA, but the other countries have not given their consent. The LACIE steering group, however

> reaffirmed an early decision to proceed with the experiment without multilateral or bilateral agreements with other wheat producing countries except Canada. The decision was taken mainly in the interest of timeliness and in consideration of the experimental nature of the undertaking. This approach also conforms to the US position of open use of space for peaceful purposes.[76]

It may be peaceful and yet not entirely innocent! Multinational grain traders are clients for LACIE-generated data and are perfectly well equipped to digest and use this information quickly. This is not always the case for other who may receive the data—not even for a State like Canada which cooperates in the program. A Canadian Member of Parliament I contacted on this question wrote to me that one problem is "the sheer quantity of information which must be processed by the user. The Canadian government official I spoke to admitted that in the joint US-Canada program, they simply were not able to digest all the data they received on US crops." The US, on the other hand, is devoting all the necessary skilled personnel to this activity and at the beginning of 1976 "USDA had assembled the *nucleus* of its LACIE staff. A total of 40 permanent and four temporary employees were on board."[77] This does not count participating experts from NASA or NOAA. Some of them have given their views on LACIE to the Press. The chief LANDSAT scientist who directs satellite data processing at NASA's Goddard base in Maryland

> emphasized that wheat data will not be used by the United States for its own economic advantages. He expressed the hope that the satellite

information eventually would become a factor in stabilizing world food prices and lead to a more equitable distribution of the crop.[78]

Some people might better stick to data-processing!

LANDSATs are not the only "spies in the skies." The most complete satellite photography is done for the CIA by the Air Force. The intelligence photos are undoubtedly much more detailed—clear down to a foot or so."[79] Firms can not only take advantage of the data collected by the US government; they can also use techniques as sophisticated as those of the Air Force for their own purposes. A new minor industry has sprung up that deals in satellite and distance photography data for agribusiness and other industrial clients. LAAD, for example, has established the Remote Sensing Engineering Ltd. (RSE) as a subsidiary whose "services are now being offered in nine Latin American countries." What remote sensing is capable of doing—if one has the money to subscribe—is phenomenal. Essentially, it "reads" and interprets electro-magnetic "signatures." "Corn, for example, has an electro-magnetic signature distinct from that of rice or bananas. Healthy corn has a different signature from diseased corn and mature corn . . . from immature corn." A sampling of services Remote Sensing Engineering can perform for its clients includes yield forecasting for any crop long before harvest "for regions or entire countries;" determination of the optimum moment for harvesting; identification of overgrazed, undergrazed or under-irrigated pastures; detection of insect infestations or plant diseases before they become visible to the naked eye, detection of plant deficiencies in any mineral nutrient; monitoring of soil humidity, salinity or erosion; plus similar services for forestry or fishery enterprises. Some of Remote Sensing's clients have included Goodyear, Upjohn pharmaceuticals, Ralston-Purina, CPC, Cargill, Central Soya and a number of large sugar estates in Central America. The company points out that its surveys are "valuable as a tool for determining inventory requirements, storage space, pricing policies, government support programs and for assisting banks with large crop-financing portfolios."[80]

The Central American peasant with a farming problem is not in the same league with Ralston Purina when it comes to access to RSE-type technology. Blight on his plot and on the neighboring estate will be detected and treated at different times—for the peasant's perhaps too late. Such services can improve yields for agribusiness and make the smallholder even less able to sustain competition. When the company explains that its services are useful for deciding "pricing policy" or "inventory requirements," the cynic may wonder if such policies and requirements cannot be used against the peasant under contract to a firm, both in times of plenty and in times of scarcity. There is a good deal of pious rhetoric to the effect that "science is free, accessible to all." This is nonsense. Knowledge costs money and tends to flow towards those who already have wealth and power; the knowledge gap is another aspect of the development gap and the class gap. Of course, satellite technology *could* be used to find locusts before they breed into swarms; it *could* help Sahelian countries map ground water resources, and maybe it will. But there is no legislation or international body governing the proliferation of private teledetection firms—much less State undertakings like LACIE—that are quite free to sell their studies on countries to agribusinesses without the knowledge or consent of the countries concerned; and certainly nothing to stop large nations like the US from making their own definitions of the "peaceful" uses of space.

Post Harvest Technology

Many people who exert influence and power inside the UN, the World Bank and other bastions of development theory and practice are still not convinced that the only way to eradicate hunger is through radical social and political change both within and between nations. Such people are therefore exceptionally receptive to the "technological fix" that promises painless progress and a solution to all the nagging problems within the existing economic and class order. The Green Revolution—the biggest post-war technological fix of them all—has proven itself a failure. One may still recommend its components, while employing a different vocabulary, but socially speaking, it is definitely out, passé. Technological fixes do not grow on trees and there has been considerable casting about for new ones since the World Food Conference. Post Harvest Technology (PHT) is a front runner and has drawn the attention of any number of distinguished development planners in recent years.

This is not to say that there is no problem of post harvest grain loss—of course there is. Its dimensions may, however, have been grossly exaggerated. Kissinger spoke of 15%, but four years later, the figures one runs across everywhere from the FAO to the popular press are commonly "20 to 40%" of UDC harvests lost in storage, handling, etc. It frequently happens that a person or an institution with good media exposure one day cites a figure which is then repeated until it becomes "fact." This is generally simple error, with no malice or conspiracy involved. Yet, at the risk of displaying here more skepticism than is warranted, I wonder if there has not been an exaggeration of losses for the furtherance of commercial interests. If it can be "proven" that peasants are lazy and hopeless at preserving their own harvests—then there is good reason for asking someone else to do it—in the present case, Western industry.

As one French scholar has put it: "There are no improvident peasants." It is indeed logical that people who have worked hard to bring in their harvest, and whose life depends upon it, are not going to leave it to the rats or insects if they can help it. Accounts of traditional village storage systems bear this out. "Granaries were an integral part and doubtless the *cornerstone* of pre-colonial agricultural systems (in the former French Sahelian colonies.")[81] Although many Western experts presented the severe Sahelian drought of the late 60's and early 70's as an extraordinary event, African peasants were accustomed to drought and to bad years and always took their likelihood into account. One particularly forthright French Colonial Inspector noted in a report on Upper Volta during the famine year 1932:

One can only wonder how it happens that populations . . . who always had on hand three harvests in reserve and to whom it was socially unacceptable to eat grain that had spent less than three years in the granary have suddenly become improvident. They managed to get through the terrible famine of 1914 without difficulty . . . (However, since the late 1920s) these populations, once rich in food reserves are now living from hand to mouth . . . [82]

The Inspector concludes that it is enforced cash crop production that has drastically reduced food crop reserves. But the point is that "backward" peasants had developed thoroughly efficient and sophisticated storage systems able to keep their grain reserves palatable for at least three years—until colonialism destroyed these practices.

Certainly much traditional knowledge has been lost because of such outside intervention; still the first step in reducing post harvest losses should be to consult the peasants themselves. FAO has a special $10 million fund to spend on PHT; the commission overseeing its spending hopes it will "give priority to actions to reduce losses at the farm and village level . . . the type of improvements introduced should be simple, practical and based on the use of local materials."[83] So much the better if they are—industry, however, already has ideas on the subject.

The Industry Cooperative Programme (ICP), until recently a part of FAO,* wanted to:

> tap the considerable ICP membership capacity . . . (and take steps to) make available advice and assistance to developing countries interested in improving their on-farm storage of food crops . . . Member capabilities in the packaging, storage, handling, transport and distribution of such foods should be brought to bear on any improved world system.[84]

Happily or unhappily, industry has nothing whatever to contribute to *on-farm* storage in UDCs. Industry has no reason to understand local requirements or the uses of local raw materials and should better leave such questions to farmers and their families (with occasional help from the State). It also seems to be the case that industry has very little to contribute to larger-scale storage schemes. One FAO official who has thoroughly studied these questions writes that "ambitious storage and processing operations in some developing countries have apparently failed to play a useful role in the post harvest systems concerned." When he gets down to particulars, we understand why. Lots of centralized storage systems—the concrete and steel kind that are supplied by industry—have been set up with total disregard for the ways in which peasant societies function. Farmers would rather have their grain close to hand, they only sell to far-off storage centers if in dire need of cash; and even if they do have surpluses to sell, the local processor can frequently offer them a better deal than the distant central facility (if only because of transport costs). Central storage is a failure because it is under-used (only to 14% of capacity in one African country) but also because the moment it *does* begin to fill up, infestations and fungi spread rapidly so that actually *more* food is often lost in "modern" post-harvest systems

---

*I am gratified to say that partly because of my own work and also thanks to the efforts of Professor Erich Jacoby of Stockholm, the Director General of the Food and Agricultural Organization (FAO), Edouard Saouma, decided in 1978 to throw the Industry Cooperative Programme (a group of over a hundred multinational agribusinesses) out of his Organization. ICP's business executive members immediately asked Secretary Waldheim for "a more central position in the UN system"; he suggested they join the United Nations Development Program (UNDP) with his blessings, but UNDP's governing Council refused them entry. A last-minute (October 1978) bulletin from Geneva informs me that a few ICP officers were then still in a UN annex, keeping their doors closed and their profiles low while searching for an agency to take the Programme in. It now seems unlikely they will find one. Mr. Saouma should be commended and Chapter 9 of my book (except as regards the Bankers Programme) should be viewed as of historical interest only.

61

than in "backward" ones. Centralized storage is also costly in terms of foreign exchange, provides almost no employment and *its use adds at least 20% to the final cost of food* to the consumer. On-farm storage, on the other hand, has a great many advantages—the farmer has experience and knowledge of local building and pest control materials, he provides his own labor, his family constantly oversees the condition of the stored grain, no money is spent on transport and next to none on capital requirements, anything that does spoil is not wasted but is fed to animals.[85]

If all this is true, why haven't the World Bank, USAID *et al.* rushed headlong into strengthening *local* storage and processing arrangements? To give them the benefit of the doubt, they perhaps do not fully understand the situation, for, as this same authority points out, very little *real* work has been done on the subject of post-harvest losses and a good bit of what has been done is inaccurate because it counts as "loss" what is really nothing but weight-reduction due to evaporation of moisture. One of the few serious studies done shows that depending on the climate of the region and the diligence of individual farmers, peasant losses actually range from 2½ to 11%.

The simplest explanation for the new vogue of Post Harvest Technology is that it costs money and can be a new market opening up for Western suppliers—the Green Revolution of the 80s, so to speak. (Incidentally, hybrid, Green Revolution grain is more delicate and more difficult to store—it may require mechanical drying and special techniques. This is one illustration of the inter-relatedness of the uniform food system—accept one part and you may be stuck with them all).

The other agribusiness connection is more tenuous, but convincing. Processing firms that set up in UDCs must be assured of regular supplies for their plants. Only centralized storage can provide these. Thus "investments in commercial storage facilities may be made by industrial processors, including those in the feed industry, in order to secure supplies and stabilize raw material costs . . . "[86]

Governments also want to be very sure they have enough food on hand in time of shortage so that they may forestall social upheavals in the cities. But they are frequently confronted with recalcitrant peasants who would rather keep their grain for their own families. "In order to resolve the dilemma (of empty central storage) a grains and legumes board in a western African country resorted to sending soldiers into villages to induce farmers to sell."[87]

The newest institution in the United Nations family, the UN University (UNU), has one program devoted to food processing and post harvest losses. Two of its earliest advisors were officers of General Foods and Campbell's Soups. The UNU recommendations on PHT are surprisingly close to those of the late Industry Cooperative Programme, e.g. "(one must) prevent, through the application of post-harvest technology, the quantitative and qualitative food losses that are estimated to be between 20 and 40% in the developing countries" (here come those figures again), so what is needed is "interdisciplinary application of science and technology and management practices in order to conserve food . . . "[88]

Nowhere is there any mention of *existing* systems (except insofar as they can be improved with "science and technology") nor is there consideration of the *cost* that expensive post harvest systems will inevitably add to food. Of the 21 members of the original UNU Expert Group, most were Western or Japanese professors of "food science and technology," only six were from the Third World, and none were women. Of the first three "associated institutions" training UNU Fellows in PHT, all are located in cities. Some good may come out of concentrating on losses and processing, but the UNU should be watched carefully to ascertain whether or not it is merely another antechamber for agribusiness.

Industrial food processing that uses machinery imported from the developed world (outside of supplying the largest cities) is not the answer for the Third World. Once again, it is too costly and puts food out of the reach of most people. It weighs on foreign exchange outflows and often doesn't even produce the sorts of basic foods that are needed. Nestle, for example, never engages in fluid milk production in UDCs but prefers condensed milk, infant formulas and other high-profit items like yogurt and ice-cream. Western processing using capital intensive techniques creates very little employment, whereas simple, labor intensive storage and processing arrangements create employment and through more employment create more demand for other goods. Any increase in food production—*if* it is processed locally, will help create jobs. For example, the International Labour Organization has shown that an extra five million tons of paddy (rice), if hand crushed, could provide employment for 870,000 people.[89]

Change Their Tastes, Change Their Minds

The last "downstream" aspect of food systems I want to mention briefly is the agribusiness effort to change tastes in order to sell more. First off, pretty soon, the whole world will be eating bread—preferably bread made from US wheat. This is a *fait accompli* in Korea where there are several mills and 7,000 bakeries; a flour mill that will require 400,000 tons of imported wheat a year is under construction in Sri Lanka where rice has always been the staple food. The Great Plains Wheat Association (GPW) made a five week trip to

Africa in 1977 to "explore specific alternatives for increased wheat market development activities in West Africa and Zaire . . . to acquaint (government) leaders with the GPW market development program."[90] Seven of the countries visited already import over 1,300,000 tons of wheat a year; they produce *nine* tons. With "the implementation of intensive market development programs in West and Central Africa, the imports of wheat to these markets should increase significantly over the next five years." In fact, GPW sees over 2 million tons in 1981-82 if all goes well. The Great Plains travelers contacted as many government planners as they could, but were not above visiting millers or even pastry-shop owners. This survey was phase one. In order "to fully achieve the goal of maximizing US wheat sales to West and Central Africa," phases two and three will require that they:

> develop personal relationships with key government, industry and business leaders in the decision making, importing and processing sectors. Identify and develop third party cooperators. These goals will be accomplished through frequent trips to the area and through the dissemination of pertinent market information by the African Regional Office. Development and implementation of pilot market development programs in selected countries (including) technical servicing of milling and baking industries and participation in trade shows.

While no stone is left unturned to increase consumption of what is a foreign food for most of the Third World, bread is not the only wheat product to be introduced. In *Global Reach,* Barnet and Muller describe the dream of National Biscuit Company's former President: to have the same satellite cracker advertisement beamed at two billion consumers at once. While we await that great day, Nabisco is busy getting Ritz crackers into every retail outlet it can find in the UDCs. The company has already launched the "largest new product venture in Nabisco's 78 year history"; four years and $15 million have been required to develop a rice-soya blend called Ricetein. "It is priced higher than rice but is less expensive than meat." Nabisco expects to sell bulk shipments, processing plants, and royalties on Ricetein to any number of poor countries where rice is the staple food. Senegal was the first to sign up—first for bulk shipments, then for the process and the plant.[91] Senegal grows rice (but no soya); Nabisco can thus help it to make its rice more expensive for the average consumer by fortifying it with protein most nutritionists would consider unnecessary. People who get enough "energy" foods (including rice) generally get enough protein as well—in any case, if there is a nutritional problem, imported US soya is not the cheapest solution.

"The battle for control of the world food system is now being waged, and its chief combatants are agribusiness and the State."

Coca Cola's strategy is the opposite of Nabisco's: it would rather have its name deeply imprinted on the consciousness of every inhabitant of the Third World even if it does not yet have any distribution in the area. Coke will spend $5 million sponsoring soccer clubs for kids in Africa and the Middle East, "even though distribution of Coke itself in many areas is miniscule or non-existent." The 14-28 year old market is the best soft-drink target and while there is no baby boom at home, in many Third World countries half the population is under 25. Coke's Latin American Director says "The only thing that's going to hold back our growth there for the next several decades is going to be a lack of machinery, trucks and equipment."[92]

White bread replaces rice and tortillas; soft drinks, because they are so expensive, replace nearly everthing, and most readers will already be aware of the great harmful influence MNC advertising has had on downgrading breastfeeding and promoting infant formula in the Third World.

US fast-food chains are already installing their first affiliates in countries of traditional agribusiness investment like Brazil and Mexico. I am not suggesting that by Friday there will be a McDonalds in Rwanda. What does seem clear is that each peripheral country, according to its station and its resources, the affluence of its population and the docility of its peasants, will find its niche in the world food system. The process will be accelerated in direct proportion to the degree of servility of the ruling elites to outside interests or their ignorance of their true aims. The battle for control of the world food system is now being waged, and its chief combatants are agribusiness and the State. From my vantage point, the odds are depressingly in favor of agribusiness.

Notes Toward A Conclusion

These last few pages are called "notes toward a conclusion" and not "conclusion" because it is manifestly impossible to deal with every aspect of an enormous subject in a document of this size. Many questions have been left unanswered or have not even been asked. These final pages are therefore largely a plea for other research to flesh out the many conclusions that might be drawn: I should be especially gratified if the suggested model provided a useful framework for others undertaking more specific work on MNCs, country studies and the like.

There are, nevertheless, certain remarks I would like to make and some are of a personal nature. The experience of publishing a first book which draws a large and sometimes passionate response is perhaps equalled only by that of having one's first baby. Like most comments on babies, most reviews tend to be fairly banal and predictable; few of them contribute to the author's intellectual progress, at least in my experience. One review of *How the Other Half Dies,* was, however, exceptionally helpful to me, in an unpredictable sort of way. It ended thus:

> Yet I find it troubling that it is the people of rich and complex countries who propose this simple vision (of a different, more just society). Diversity in diet and culture seem to me to be unconditional goods. And they are goods which prosperity buys. The question suggested to me by both books is still how to use well the prosperity of the West.*

I read this over several times, trying to understand exactly what was meant. To me, too, diversity in diet and culture seem to be unconditional goods. What does Western prosperity have to do with them? The more I reflected on this, the more I felt that the reviewer was dead wrong. Those two terms—"Western prosperity" and "diversity" kept clashing in my head. Eventually, dialectics prevailed and they merged into the idea of a world food system, of increasing food *uniformity* brought about under the leadership of the West, especially that of agribusiness. Western prosperity (i.e. transnational capital) *swallows up diversity. It has no use for culture, but needs only consumers.* It does not even need peasants, which is why so many of them have become redundant.

*Emma Rothschild, "The Politics of Hunger" (a review of *Food First* and *How the Other Half Dies*); *New York Times Book Review*. 17 July 1977.

An American friend, commenting on this study, finally explained to me what the review had actually meant:

> Certainly Western prosperity does *not* swallow up diversity, as one can observe at local overstocked supermarkets. This struck me the first time I entered one upon returning from Africa. I was overwhelmed by the abundance of 'overchoice,' to borrow Alvin Toffler's term from *Future Shock*. The store shelved eighty-five kinds of bottled salad dressing. Eighty-five kinds.

If this is "diversity of diet," who needs it? Even more to the point, who can afford it? It is certainly not "diversity of culture," but the merest commercialism, attempting to drive out anything resembling personal, community or even national initiative.

There *is* a New International Economic Order being set up in the area of food, but it is agribusiness' and not the one the Third World has been negotiating for. If these basic ideas are not clear by now, it is my fault, not the reader's, but cannot in any case be remedied at this stage. That is why I want to devote the remainder of these notes not to repetition or summary but to clarification and to one or two remarks concerning positive policy.

First of all, some things I am *not* saying. I am not proposing Instant Nostalgia as a solution, a return to some totally imaginary Eden and ancestral methods. I do not share the desire of many fed-up Westerners to go raise sheep in the provinces and I am not suggesting that the Third World use . . . *simpler* agricultural systems. In fact, it seems to me that the Western system is linear, crude and not very scientific in the richest sense of the word. I would indeed like to see *much more complex* agricultural/food systems in UDCs; the kind that only the availability of many hands can make possible. This is such an important point that it will figure substantially in my future research and writing.

In spite of some evidence to the contrary, I further do not believe in conspiracy as a theory of history, nor that events are the result of a permanent plot of the rich against the poor. One can simultaneously believe in good will of many individual people working in the develoment Establishment and in the harmful effects they have *as a class* on other people's lives. I cannot say whether this is because of willful decision at the topmost levels or simply because the decision makers are so immersed in their own ideology that they are incapable of imagining viable alternatives. What one can say with certainty is that "everything takes place *as if*" the desire to foster Western interests at the expense of the Third World were the driving force behind almost all "development efforts" including "charitable" or "disinterested" interventions. The odds seem to me that this will remain the case and

67

that we must therefore take this tendency to harm—deliberate or not—into account. Future modifications brought to Third World food systems are not exempt from it.

The Transnational Institute is a community of scholar-activists; it is therefore perhaps not out of place that a few suggestions for positive action appear at the end of a TNI study whose first purpose is to inform and to convince.

First of all, groups and individuals in the industrialized countries who hope to "do something" should be concentrating, I think, on two basic lines of action, depending on their location, circumstances, particular bent, etc. One is to weaken the agribusiness chain described above at home. What weakens it in the West will also make it more vulnerable, less able to advance in the Third World. The other is to help strengthen those groups in UDCs that are working for change in their own societies. Non-governmental organizations (NGOs) can here usually be more effective than State-run development projects. Because they are smaller, they can be more imaginative, more innovative and above all more radical. The worst they need fear is outstanding success—i.e. that the local government fears their activity, wants to prevent its spread, and throws them out. A victory of sorts; some seeds may have been planted. NGO projects can also provide an embarrassing yardstick against which official development efforts may be measured. (Why doesn't USAID encourage local participation like X?) States, even repressive ones, must eventually respond to political pressures. Whether at home or abroad, we can try to diminish the power and prestige of oppressors and to help people struggling to build up their own weight in the balance of power—while always remembering that we can get on the next plane home in time of crisis, whereas the local workers and peasants cannot.

In addition, we need many more researchers in the field and some substantial money to make sure people doing good work in the developed and underdeveloped countries alike are in touch with each other and can effectively communicate their findings. Food is now becoming a somewhat fashionable field, a welcome development because one might accurately say that the number of people engaged in critical research is significantly smaller than the executive staff of any major multinational food corporation. We also need people on the inside, some means of countering the effective information networks of the companies.

This is not to imply that "development" or "food" research is the major battleground—because that, of course, is in the Third World itself. Yet one can occasionally furnish better arms to those groups that are trying to change the *status quo* in their own societies. To this extent, good development research can be dangerous to the Establishment, and, because it represents a danger, it will be fought. One of the opposition's most frequently used tactics is the accusation that such research is not "value-free" and is thus "unscientific." "Value-free" social science is a myth, but a convenient one since it considers defense and illustration of the *status quo* as "objective" and "scientific": whereas to question or to condemn the dominant system is to be "ideologically motivated." People working in the field will inevitably be faced with such accusations and should try to accept once and for all that all good development research done in the future will be value-loaded and political, because politics conditions the very questions we ask and determines our unstated assumptions. If we make no enemies, we should question the worth of our work.

This idea that research can somehow be value-free stems, it seems to me, from another prevalent myth about the development process itself. The theories of "GNP growth" and "trickle-down" rest upon this myth, which assumes, for mysterious reasons, that the UDC classes that have gained wealth and power will want to share both with their less fortunate countrymen. Have we in the West such short memories that we cannot even recall the fact that our own enjoyment of *relatively* more egalitarian societies is not due to the benevolence or the largesse of our own dominant classes but has been achieved through decades and centuries of struggle—struggles of farmers and workers and women and minorities? Why should it be any different in the Third World? Why should one assume that "development" will be a harmonious process, somehow exempt from conflict? Development *is* conflict, and there are real forces opposing it; real enemies with real interests who are not playing games. Neither must we.

Now that "trickle-down" as a solution has been largely discredited by the facts themselves, there is a need for new strategies, or at least for new slogans. Two of these are "Basic Needs" and "Self-Reliance." No one can be *against* satisfying basic needs, but there are dangers inherent in the slogan if it is used in the wrong way. If it is merely excuse for the army of development cadres to go out and measure and weigh and photograph and calibrate the perennial "target-groups" of the Third World; in order to determine how many calories and pairs of shoes and hours of education they need, we may as well forget it. It is the "target-groups" that ought to be targeting the experts, telling them what their needs are and the obstacles they see to satisfying them. It is rare that they are asked to do so. Basic needs are not merely physical but involve also that nebulous "quality of life" that no group has a right to define for any other. One must also question how those needs are to be satisfied—by people themselves, working in community or larger groups? Or in some mysterious way by the "market" which has not shown to date marked ability to provide bare essentials? "Basic Needs" is going to be served up with a variety of sauces, and we must be on the lookout for those that are adulterated.

"Self-reliance," again, is attractive, also becoming fashionable, to the point that one can hear some Third World leaders say, in effect, "To become self-reliant, we need to import X, Y or Z." Real self-reliance does not mean autarchy, but it does imply a certain class structure, a particular relationship between the leaders and the people. It cannot be achieved in any significant measure when their interests diverge. Some leaders may try to hide greater hardship and exploitation of the peasantry under the cloak of self-reliance. The example of Cambodia comes to mind, although one should not make definitive judgments on the amount of information presently available.

There are some brave souls inside the development Establishment genuinely trying to encourage political change of the kind that comes about only through real popular participation (even inside the World Bank). The furthest-reaching critique of current development research and practices coming from an official body is doubtless that of the United Nations Research Institute for Social Development (UNRISD) which goes beyond "Basic Needs" by posing the double requirement of *livelihood* and *participation* as the criteria for real development.* Livelihood is not merely so many calories or yards of cloth or tons of bricks, whatever their importance, but involves cultural values; just as participation is not causing people to acquiesce to decisions made for them elsewhere but a political stance holding that people should be the subjects, not the objects of decisions that shape their lives.

The adoption of a "New Economic Order" based on the uniform food system model which guarantees Western-style standards of living for some just as surely as it does hunger for others is probably the line of least resistance most Third World countries will follow. The only way to oppose it is through genuine political commitment, backed by the entire national community, which recognizes dependency as the enemy. I have tried to show how some of the mechanisms of this food system work, but this should not be construed as demonstrating their inevitability. Knowledge can act as a depressant and lead to despair, but action for and with others is liberating. We should remember Gramsci's "Optimism of the will, pessimism of the mind" and know that both for us and for the Third World, there is a choice.

*See UNRISD, *Strategy and Programme Proposals,* UNRISD 77/C. 37, Board S.S. 1977/W.P. 2/Rev. 1, Geneva, 4 November 1977.

Glossary

FAO: Food and Agriculture Organization of the United Nations

LACIE: Large Area Crop Inventory Experiment: a satellite crop surveillance program of the USDA (see below)

MNC: Multinational Corporation

NIEO: New International Economic Order

OPIC: Overseas Private Investment Corporation; the US government agency which provides loans and insurance for US business-abroad.

PHT: Post Harvest Technology

UDC: Underdeveloped Country

UNCTAD: United Nations Conference on Trade and Development; particularly concerned with UDC agricultural raw materials and commodities

UNU: United Nations University

USAID: United States Agency for International Development

USDA: United States Department of Agriculture

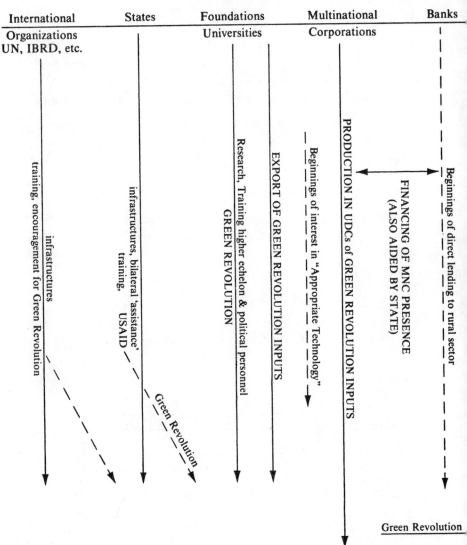

DEVELOPED COUNTRIES
USA

INPUTS
UPSTREAM ──────────→

FARM PRODUCTION
+ 4% US population

International	States	Foundations	Multinational	Banks
Organizations UN, IBRD, etc.		Universities	Corporations	

training, encouragement for Green Revolution

infrastructures

infrastructures, bilateral 'assistance' training, USAID

Green Revolution

Research, Training higher echelon & political personnel
GREEN REVOLUTION

EXPORT OF GREEN REVOLUTION INPUTS

Beginnings of interest in "Appropriate Technology"

PRODUCTION IN UDCs of GREEN REVOLUTION INPUTS

FINANCING OF MNC PRESENCE
(ALSO AIDED BY STATE)

Beginnings of direct lending to rural sector

Green Revolution

PRESENCE OF MNCs in UDCs

UNDERDEVELOPED COUNTRIES

UPSTREAM Green Revolution inputs do not reach small cultivators ──────────→

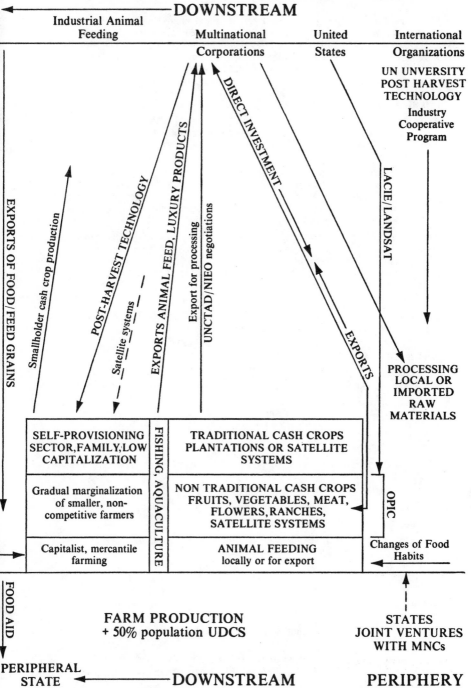

References Part I

1.   For a history of the struggle for the NIEO, see Orlando Letelier and Michael Moffitt; *The International Economic Order,* TNI Pamphlet No. 2, Washington, D.C., 1977. Also Sylvain Minault; *The New International Economic Order: The Promise and the Reality,* Friends World Committee for Consultation, London 1977. Details of proposed commodity agreements will be found in the UNCTAD document, *An Integrated Programme for Commodities,* Report of the Secretary General of UNCTAD (TD/B/C.1/166) and the five supplements to this report. Another useful source is Barbara Huddleston, *Commodity Trade Issues in International Negotiations,* International Food Policy Research Institute, Washington, D.C. 1977. See also notes 2 and 4.

2.   George Eads, quoted in Jere R. Behrman; *International Commodity Agreements: An evaluation of the UNCTAD Integrated Commodity Programme,* Overseas Development Council Monograph no. 9, Washington, D.C. 1977, p. 2-3.

3.   Behrman, idem, sp. pp. x-xi, p. 34, pp. 38-39. The quotation (p. 39) is based on C. Fred Bergsten; "The Policy of the United States Toward International Commodity Agreements," Statement by Assistant Secretary of the Treasury for International Affairs before the Subcommittee on Economic Stabilization of the House Committee on Banking, Finance and Urban Affairs, June 1977.

4.   The World Bank; *World Tables 1976* ("Social Indicators"). Table 3, p. 514-17; all figures for 1970. If control of *capital*—not just income—were included, the concentration of wealth in the hands of the top 5% would show up much more strongly and the apparently greater equality of distribution in the US and Canada would of course be sharply reduced.

5.   Behrman, op. cit. Table 13.

6.   Calculated from data in Helen O'Neill, *A Common Interest in a Common Fund,* United Nations, New York 1977, Annex p. 44.

7.   See "Can Agriculture Save the Dollar?" *Forbes,* 15 March 1973. Agricultural exports represent an average 20% of total US exports.

8.   Chase Economic Consulting Service, *Confidential Report to Executives:* "Special Forecast: The Long-Term Outlook for US Agriculture," New York, October 1977.

9.   United States Department of Agriculture; *Market Potential for US Agricultural Commodities in Select Mid-East and North African Countries;* USDA-FAS; FAS M-269, October 1975 and Foreign Agriculture Circular, *World Grain Situation,* USDA FG 2-78, p. 9-10.

10.   *US Foreign Agricultural Trade Statistical Report,* Calendar Year 1976, Table 34, p. 338.

11.   Calculated from data in idem, Tables 3 and 21.

12.   Idem, Table 25, sp. pp. 316 and 318.

13.   Idem, Table 21, sp. from pp. 229-237.

14.   "New Corn Derivative Challenges Big Sugar as Shakeout Looms," *Wall Street Journal,* 2 November 1976.

15.   Robert N. McConnell, Director, Sugar and Tropical Products Division, USDA-FAS; "The International Setting for Sugar and Sweeteners," Paper presented at the 1978 Food and Agriculture Outlook Conference, November 1977. Related data also in Thomas W. Little & Fred Gray; "US Sugar and Sweetener Outlook," same USDA conference, published in same USDA mimeographed series.

16.   "A Source of Natural Rubber in our own Back Yard," *Fortune,* 24 April 1978, p. 80.

17.   Dick Griffin, "Natural Rubber has a Future After All, *Fortune,* idem, p. 81.

18.   "What and Who Makes Cargill So Powerful," *Forbes,* 18 September 1978 and *Food Product Development,* cover articles for June and September 1977.

19.   Both quotes from the UNCTAD Resolution adopted on 30 May 1976, Nairobi. (TD/RES/93 (IV).)

20.   This observation includes the area of food aid, which is reduced when export prices rise and one of whose aims is the creation of commercial markets. See Susan George, *How the Other Half Dies,* chapter 8.

21.   As noted on Table, source for data is *World Bank: World Tables 1976.* "Economic Data Sheet no. 1" for the percentage of agriculture in GDP; "Economic Data Sheet no. 2" for current expenditure on defense and agriculture. Sheet no. 2 also gives data on "capital expenditure on agriculture," but since these figures include loans and grants from outside sources such as the World Bank, the UNDP, etc. who themselves decide how the money is to be spent, they do not seem to me to reflect the real priorities of governments as well as do current expenditure figures. World Bank statistics are probably more reliable than others; unfortunately they are also usually old.

22.   Dr. Moises Behar, World Health Organization, oral communication at the FAO/Scandinavian Journalists Encounter, Oslo, December 1977.

23.   Siepko H. Lok; "Smallholders' Rubber Production," *Monthly Bulletin of Agricultural Economics and Statistics,* FAO, Vol. 26, no. 3, March 1977.

24.   "Inflation Bites Chocolate Again," *Business Week,* 29 August 1977.

References Part II

1.   For a more thorough discussion of the implications of cash-crop agriculture, readers are referred to my own book and to Joseph Collins and Frances Moore-Lappé, *Food First,* Houghton Mifflin, Boston 1977.

2.   This is why the United Nations Research Institute for Social Development's (UNRISD) recently designed research program "Food Systems and Society" comes as a welcome change. By the summer of 1978 work had begun in Africa, India and China; the entire study will span several years and cover a wide variety of geographical areas and academic disciplines. See *Food Systems and Society: Problems of food security in the modern world,* UNRISD, Project proposal, 16th Special Session of the Board, Geneva, UNRISD 78/C. 14.

3.   My doctoral dissertation for the Ecole des Hautes Etudes en Sciences Sociales, University of Paris; *Stratégies d'Intervention des Pays Industrialisés dans les Systèmes Alimentaires des Pays Périphériques,* deals extensively with these trends. I do not recommend it to anyone lacking fluent French but would be willing to make it available on a "need to know" basis at photocpy cost. The need should be pressing as there are 500 pages and photocopying is expensive in France. Inquiries may be directed to me through TNI.

4.   Those who want a detailed and lively description of the US food system should read Jim Hightower, *Eat Your Heart Out,* Crown, New York, 1975.

5.   A careful and fascinating account of the role of farm machinery and other changes will be found in Peter Dorner, "Transformation of US Agriculture: The Past Forty Years," Agricultural Economics Staff Paper Series no. 126, College of Agricultural and Life Sciences, University of Wisconsin, Madison, June 1977.

6.   John E. Lee, Jr.; "Agricultural Finance, Situation and Issues," Paper presented at the 1978 Food and Agricultural Outlook Conference, USDA, Washington, D.C., November 1977 (mimeo).

Also, "A Bumper Crop of Loans to Farmers," *Business Week,* February 28, 1977.

7.   David Lins, "Credit and Finance Outlook," Paper presented at same conference cf. note 6.

8.   "How the Family Farm can Harvest Millions," *Business Week,* July 4, 1977.

9.   Hearings before the subcommittee on family farms, rural development and special studies, Committee on Agriculture of the House of Representatives, February 18, 24, 25, 1977, pp. 45-48.

10.   Statement of Paula S. Schaedlich, Agriculture and food marketing project, Iowa public interest research group, in *Hearings*, idem. p. 333.

11.   Hightower, op. cit. p. 144.

12.   Idem, chapter 8.

13.   "Hybrid Wheat: Big New Outlet for Fertiliser?" *Chemical Week*, August 28, 1974.

14.   John E. Lee, Jr.; op. cit., Table 2, p. 12.

15.   Susan Sechler and Susan de Marco, "Earl Butz's Legacy to Farmers," *The Elements*, March 1977.

16.   Peter Dorner, op. cit. p. 9ff. Dorner is well aware that "small farmer" will mean different things in different contexts. In Wisconsin, he sets the cut-off, no-go line for dairy farms purchased after 1950 at about 80 acres; for corn/soybeans, 160 acres, for wheat, 320 acres.

17.   Linda Grant Martin, "How Beatrice Foods Sneaked up on $5 Billion," *Fortune*, April 1976.

18.   Tables on Research and Development Spending, 1977, *Business Week*, July 3, 1977, p. 65ff.

19.   A good example is Textured Vegetable Protein which comes in flakes, grains, minces, globs or what-have-you and is a very hot item on the food processing scene. It is made from soya, so does not qualify as ersatz on grounds of origin, but the extrusion technology involved relates it more to an organic chemical. See also Hightower, op. cit. p. 108f.

20.   Daniel Zwerdling, "The Food Monopolies," *The Progressive*, January 1975.

21.   Walter Keichel, III; "The Soggy Case Against the Cereal Industry," *Fortune*, April 10, 1978.

22.   USDA-Economic Research Service: "Contract production and vertical integration in farming, 1960 and 1970," Report no. 479, April 1972, pp. 4-5 (reproduced in a working document of the United Nations Center on Transnational Corporations.)

23.   Hightower, op. cit., p. 165.

24.   For a brilliant exposition of the reasons why capitalist production of all kinds is *necessarily* wasteful, one can do no better than to read or re-read Baran and Sweezy's classic *Monopoly Capital*, Monthly Review Press, New York 1966. They do not discuss agribusiness, but the concepts apply.

25.   Full explanation plus 85 "energy budgets" in Gerald Leach, *Energy and Food Production*, IPC Science and Technology Press, Guildford (Surrey, UK) 1976.

26.   *Alternative Futures for US Agriculture: A Progress Report;* prepared by the USDA Office of Planning and Evaluation for the Committee on Agriculture and Forestry, US Senate, Washington, D.C. GPO, September 1975.

27.   Idem, Tables 11, 29, 44 and 24.

28.   Idem, p. 33.

29.   Howard Kunreuther, "Why the Poor May Pay More for Food: Theoretical and Empirical Evidence," *Journal of Business*, University of Chicago, July 1973.

30.   *Proceedings* of the Sub-committee on National Security Policy and Scientific Development of the Committee on Foreign Affairs, House of Representatives, December 5, 1969, p. 127.

31.   Idem, p. 36. Pierre Spitz has analyzed Foundations' roles in detail in *De la Recherche en Sciences Sociales du Développement aux Etats-Unis*, Institut National de la Recherche Agronomique, Paris 1971 (mimeo); I have borrowed from him here.

32.   Arthur T. Mosher, President of the Agricultural Development Council, testifying in *Proceedings, p. 73*.

33.   Garrison Wilkes, "The World's Crop Plant Germ Plasm: An Endangered Resource," *The Bulletin of the Atomic Scientists*, February 1977, p. 15-16.

34.   Idem, p. 16.

35.   "A Rich Harvest for Seed Growers," *Business Week,* January 13, 1975.

36.   J.I. Hendrie, Head, Life Sciences, Shell International Chemical Co., Ltd. "Seed Production and Plant Breeders' Rights." Paper prepared for the Consultation with Agro-Industrial Leaders in Preparation for the World Food Conference, Toronto, September 1974.

37.   M. Kreisberg, "Miracle Seeds and Market Economies," *Columbia Journal of World Business,* March-April 1969.

38.   "India: What Can We Do to Help?" *JD Journal* (John Deere), Moline, Illinois, Vol. 3 no. 4 (1974).

39.   K.N. Raj, "La mécanisation de l'agriculture en Inde et à Sri Lanka," *Revue Internationale de Travail* (International Labor Office), Geneva, October 1972. Raj also quotes from S.R. Bose, "The Green Revolution and Agricultural Employment under Conditions of Rapid Population Growth." Retranslated into English by SG.

40.   K.C. Abercrombie, "Agricultural Employment in Latin America," *International Labor Organization Review,* July 1972.

41.   Both quotes from Solon Barraclough and Jacobo Schatan; "Technological Change and Agricultural Development," *Land Economics* (Univeristy of Wisconsin), May 1973, p. 188.

42.   Andrew Pearse, "Technology and Peasant Production: Reflections on a Global Study," *Development and Change,* (8), 1977, p. 140.

43.   Michael Lipton, speech as summarized in "Summary. Record," FAO Bankers Programme General Committee Meeting, October 21-22, 1976, (mimeo), p 5.

44.   FAO Press Releases 76/31 and 75/76.

45.   Andrew Pearse, *The Social and Economic Implications of Large-Scale Introduction of New Varieties of Food Grain: An Overview Report,* UNRISD 75/C. 11, GE75-5363, Part III, p. 5.

46.   Lester Brown with Erik P. Eckholm, "Buying time with the Green Revolution," Du Pont *Context* (no. 4, 1974) E.I. du Pont de Nemours & Co.

47.   X. *World Bank Memorandum* on India, May 5, 1975. The memorandum relies partially for its figures on successive Indian land censuses of 1961 and 1971. I shall leave the author his anonymity, but ignore the "Not for Quotation" stricture.

48.   The Asian Development Bank report is quoted in Patrice de Beer, "Les Echecs d'une Politique anti-Subversive en Asie," *Le Monde Diplomatique,* January 1978.

49.   Andrew Pearse op. cit. note 42.

50.   OPIC Computer Print-out: "Agricultural Contracts of Insurance as of December 31, 1977" and OPIC Annual Reports from 1973 to 1977.

51.   Robert J. Ledogar, *Hungry for Profits,* IDOC, New York 1976, Sp. pp. 94-98.

52.   Paul Cornelsen, President of Ralston Purina International, quoted in Harvard Business School, *Ralston Purina International,* Case 4-371-501-AI 310, p. 8-10.

53.   LAAD Annual Report 1974 ("Letter to the Shareholders").

54.   LAAD Annual Reports 1974 and 1975, "Notes to Consolidated Financial Statements."

55.   John Liston and Lynwood Smith, "Fishing and the Fishing Industry: an Account with Comments on Overseas Technology Transfers," *Ocean Development and International Law: the Journal of Marine Affairs,* Fall 1974.

56.   World Food Program Press Release 78/25/WFP/29; FAO Press Releases 78/43/CO/8 and 78/49/CO/11.

57.   cf. "Ralston Purina Profits by Going to the Dogs," *Commercial and Financial Chronicle,* June 17, 1974.

58.   M. Merlier, "Le Congo de la Colonisation Belge à l'Independance," Maspero, Paris 1963. Cited in M.K.K. Kabala Kabunda, "Multinational Corporations and the

Installation of Externally Oriented Economic Structures in Contemporary Africa" in Carl Widstrand, ed. *Multinational Firms in Africa,* Scandinavian Institute for African Studies, Uppsala 1975, p. 305-06.

59. Lord Cole in the *Financial Times* of May 28, 1966, cited in Counter Information Service, *Unilever's World,* Anti-Report no. 11, p. 93.

60. Xavier Browaeys, "Le Commerce International des Oleagineux et des Matieres Grasses," *L'Information Géographique,* November-December 1973, p. 235.

61. Peter Nehemkis, "Expropriation has a Silver Lining," *California Management Review,* Fall 1974.

62. For a detailed account of Nestle's Third World activities, see Susan George, "Nestle Alimentana S.A.: The Limits to Public Relations," *Economic and Political Weekly,* (Bombay), XIII, September 16, 1978, pp. 1591-1602.

63. OPIC Annual Report 1976, p. 38-39. There is no way I have found to tell what capital sources or MNC the name "Tea Importers Inc." conceals. The International Finance Corporation, the World Bank affiliate that engages in private investment, lists this same operation under the name "Societe Rwandaise du Thé, SARL" and merely says that in addition to OPIC, "equity capital was provided by the private US sponsor and local investors." IFC Annual Report 1976, p. 19. Just as a matter of general interest, OPIC also insures a bank set up in Rwanda by Morgan Guaranty.

64. Bernard Roux, "Expansion du Capitalisme et Developpement du Sous-Développement: L'Intégration de l'Amérique Centrale dans le Marché Mondial de la Viande Bovine." *Revue du Tiers Monde,* IEDES-PUF, Paris, April-June 1975.

N.B. Roux's figures extend only to the end of 1972; the situation has grown much worse since then.

65. Ray A. Goldberg, *Agribusiness Management for Developing Countries—Latin America,* Ballinger, Cambridge (Mass.), 1974.

66. Idem, Table 4-6, p. 160-61.

67. Idem, p. 178.

68. Idem, p. 202.

69. Idem, p. 158-59, p. 195.

70. Idem, p. 272, p. 289.

71. Ernst Feder, *Strawberry Imperialism: An Enquiry into the Mechanisms of Dependency in Mexican Agriculture,* Institute of Social Studies, The Hague, 1976.

72. Details of Sinaloa growing operations in NACLA, "Harvest of Anger," *Latin America and Empire Report,* Vol X, no. 6, July-August 1976.

73. Ray A. Goldberg, "Agribusiness for Developing Countries," *Harvard Business Review,* September-October 1966.

74. e.g. Thomas Horst, *At Home Abroad,* Ballinger, Cambridge (Mass.) 1974; Henry J. Frundt, *American Agribusiness and US Foreign Policy,* Doctoral thesis, Rutgers University, 1975.

75. Large Area Crop Inventory Experiment (LACIE) *1976 Year-End Report to USDA Executive Steering Group and Participating USDA Agencies,* January 31, 1977 (mimeo), p. 1.

76. Idem, p. 2-3.

77. Idem ,my emphasis.

78. "US Plans Satellite Survey to Predict Wheat Harvests," *International Herald Tribune,* January 12, 1977.

79. James Ridgeway, "Spy in the Sky," *The Elements,* May 1975.

80. Quotes are from an undated brochure of Remote Sensing Engineering, Ltd.

81. J. Egg, F. Lerin, M. Venin; *Analyse Descriptive de la Famine des Années 1931 au Niger,* Institut National de la Recherche Agronomique (INRA) Paris, 1975, p. 28, p. 52, their emphasis.

82.   Laurence Wilhelm, "Le Rôle et la Dynamique de l'Etat à travers les Crises de Subsistence: Le Cas de la Haute Volta," *Mémoire de Thèse,* ⁚ Institut des Etudes du Développement, Geneva, October 1976; cited in Pierre Spitz, "Silent Violence: Famine and Inequality," in *Violence and Its Causes,* UNESCO, Division of Human Rights and Peace, forthcoming 1979.

83.   FAO Press Release 77/116/C/19.

84.   Draft notes of the Deliberations of Panel C on World Food Security, Consultation with Agro-Industrial Leaders in Preparation for the World Food Conference, Toronto, September 1974.

85.   E. Reuss, "Economic and Marketing Aspects of Post Harvest Systems in Small Farmer Economies" (a two-part article), *FAO Monthly Bulletin of Agricultural Economics and Statistics,* Vol. 25, nos. 9 and 10 (September and October 1976).

86.   Idem, Part I, p. 4.

87.   Idem, p. 5.

88.   Report of the United Nations University Expert Group on World Hunger, September 22-26, 1975 (mimeo) p. 11.

89.   International Labour Organization, Second Tri-Partite Meeting for the Food Processing and Drinks Industry, Technical Report no. 3: "Appropriate Technology for Employment Generation in the Food Processing and Drinks Industries of Developing Countries," Chapter 3, ILO, Geneva 1977.

90.   Photocopy of Great Plains Wheat Association; *Trip Report: African Wheat Market Survey* (May 30-July 6, 1977) typescript.

91.   "Let 'em Eat Ricetein," *Forbes,* May 1, 1976 and "Senegal to get New Protein Food Developed in US," *International Herald Tribune,* April 10-11, 1976.

92.   "The Greying of the Soft Drink Industry," *Business Week,* May 23, 1977.

IPS PUBLICATIONS

Dubious Specter:
A Skeptical Look
at the 'Soviet Threat'
By Fred Kaplan

A thorough exposition and analysis of the myths and realities surrounding the current U.S.-Soviet "military balance." Kaplan's comparisons of U.S. and Soviet nuclear arsenals and strategies provide the necessary background for understanding current debates on arms limitations and rising military costs. $4.95.

The Rise and Fall
of the 'Soviet Threat':
Domestic Sources of the
Cold War Consensus
By Alan Wolfe

A timely essay which demonstrates that American fear of the Soviet Union tends to fluctuate due to domestic factors, not in relation to the military and foreign policies of the USSR. Wolfe contends that recurring features of American domestic politics periodically coalesce to spur anti-Soviet sentiment, contributing to increased tensions and dangerous confrontations. $4.95.

Resurgent Militarism
By Michael T. Klare
and the Bay Area Chapter
of the Inter-University Committee

An analysis of the origins and consequences of the growing militaristic fervor which is spreading from Washington across the nation. The study examines America's changing strategic position since Vietnam and the political and economic forces which underlie the new upsurge in militarism. $2.00.

The Counterforce Syndrome:
A Guide to U.S. Nuclear Weapons
and Strategic Doctrine
By Robert C. Aldridge

An identification of how "counterforce" has replaced "deterrence" as the Pentagon's prevailing doctrine, contrary to what most Americans believe. This thorough summary and analysis of U.S. strategic nuclear weapons and military doctrine includes descriptions of MIRVs, MARVs, Trident systems, cruise missiles, and M-X missiles as they relate to the aims of a U.S. first strike. $4.95.

The Giants
Russia and America
By Richard Barnet

An authoritative, comprehensive account of the latest stage of the complex U.S.-Soviet relationship; how it came about, what has changed, and where it is headed.

"A thoughtful and balanced account of American-Soviet relations. Barnet goes beyond current controversies to discuss the underlying challenges of a relationship that is crucial to world order." —Cyril E. Black, Director, Center for International Studies, Princeton University

"An extraordinarily useful contribution to the enlightenment of the people of this country .... It is of fundamental importance that we understand the true state of our relations with Russia if we are to avoid a tragic mistake in our future."—Senator J.W. Fulbright. $4.95.

The New Generation
of Nuclear Weapons
By Stephen Daggett

An updated summary of strategic weapons, including American and Soviet nuclear hardware. These precarious new technologies may provoke startling shifts in strategic policy, leading planners to consider fighting "limited nuclear wars" or consider a preemptive first strike capability. $2.00.

Toward World Security:
A Program for Disarmament
By Earl C. Ravenal

This proposal argues that in light of destabilizing new strategic weapons systems and increasing regional conflicts which could involve the superpowers, the U.S. should take independent steps toward disarmament by not deploying new "counterforce" weapons, pledging no first use of nuclear weapons, and by following a non-interventionist foreign policy. $2.00.

Peace In Search of Makers
Riverside Church Reverse
the Arms Race Convocation
Jane Rockman, Editor

A compilation of papers denouncing the proliferation of sophisticated weaponry, which threatens a nuclear cataclysm and destroys our society by diverting resources from social services and programs. This volume confronts the moral, economic, strategic and ethical aspects of the arms race and appeals for a citizen coalition to reverse the course of social decay and uncontrolled nuclear armament. Contributions by Richard Barnet, Michael Klare, Cynthia Arnson, Marcus Raskin and others. $5.95.

Assassination on Embassy Row
By John Dinges and Saul Landau

A devastating political document that probes all aspects of the Letelier-Moffitt assassinations, interweaving the investigations of the murder by the FBI and the Institute. The story surpasses the most sophisticated fiction in depth of characterization at the same time that it raises serious and tantalizing questions about the response of American intelligence and foreign policy to international terrorism. $14.95.

Supplying Repression:
U.S. Support for
Authoritarian Regimes Abroad
By Michael T. Klare

A description of how the U.S. continues to supply arms and training to police and other internal security forces of repressive governments abroad. "Very important, fully documented indictment of U.S. role in supplying rightist Third World governments with the weaponry and know-how of repression."—*The Nation.* $4.95.

After the Shah
By Fred Halliday

Important background information on the National Front, the Tudeh Party, the religious opposition and many other groups whose policies and programs will determine Iran's future. $2.00.

A Continent Beseiged:
Foreign Military Activities
in Africa Since 1975
By Daniel Volman

A study of the growing military involvement of the two superpowers and their allies in Africa. Challenging the usual exclusive focus on Soviet and Cuban activities, the study suggests that the continuing escalation of French and American involvement threatens to engulf the continent in armed chaos and to bring the two superpowers into direct confrontation. Contains extensive data on African arms trade, the strength of African military forces, and the role of foreign military personnel. $2.00.

The Lean Years
Politics in the Age of Scarcity
By Richard J. Barnet

A lucid and startling analysis of basic global resources: energy, non-fuel minerals, food, water, and human labor. The depletion and maldistribution of supplies bodes a new global economic, political and military order in the 1980s.

" . . . brilliantly informed book . . . cogent, aphoristic pulling together of the skeins of catastrophic scarcity in 'the coming postpetroleum world' . . . "—*Publishers Weekly*. $12.95.

Feeding the Few:
Corporate Control of Food
By Susan George

The author of *How the Other Half Dies* has extended her critique of the world food system which is geared toward profit not people. This study draws the links between the hungry at home and those abroad exposing the economic and political forces pushing us towards a unified global food system. $4.95.

How the Other Half Dies
By Susan George

This important examination of multinational agribusiness corporations explains that the roots of hunger are not over-population, changing climate, or bad weather, but rather the control of food by the rich.

"A most intelligent, urgent and thought-provoking book on a truly vital subject."—*John Kenneth Galbraith*. $5.95.

Human Rights, Economic Aid
and Private Banks:
The Case of Chile
By Michael Moffitt and Isabel Letelier

This issue paper documents the tremendous increase in private bank loans to the Chilean military dictatorship since the overthrow of Salvador Allende in 1973. Previously unpublished data demonstrates how private banks rescued the Chilean military government by increasing loans to Chile at the very time governments and international institutions were reducing their loans because of massive human rights violations. $2.00.

Decoding Corporate Camouflage:
U.S. Business Support
for Apartheid
By Elizabeth Schmidt

By exposing the decisive role of U.S. corporations in sustaining apartheid, this study places highly-touted employment "reforms" in the context of the systematic economic exploitation and political repression of the black South African majority. Schmidt charges that the Sullivan Principles—the fair employment code devised by American corporations to deflect public criticism of their South African activities—are scanty cover for U.S. capital, technology, and know-how that support the white minority regime.
" . . .forcefully presented."—Kirkus Reviews. $4.95.

South Africa:
Foreign Investment and Apartheid
By Lawrence Litvak, Robert DeGrasse,
Kathleen McTigue

A critical examination of the argument that multinationals and foreign investment are a force for progressive change in South Africa. This study carefully documents the role that foreign investment has played in sustaining apartheid. $3.95.

Black South Africa Explodes
By Counter Information Services

The only detailed account available of events in South Africa in the first year since the uprising which began in June 1976 in Soweto. The report exposes the reality of life in the African townships, the impact of South Africa's economic crisis on blacks, and the white regime's dependence on European and American finance. $2.95.

The New Gnomes:
Multinational Banks in the Third World
By Howard M. Wachtel

This work documents and analyzes the growth of Third World debt to private U.S.-based multinational banks, and the impact of this new form of indebtedness on the politics and economic policies of Third World countries. $4.95.

Common Sense for Hard Times
By Jeremy Brecher and Tom Costello

Inflation, unemployment, declining real incomes, environmental degradation, powerlessness at work and away—these are the basic problems that face most people right now. This valuable book tells in practical terms how we can deal with them effectively.

"A popularly written analysis of modern times . . . a primer on class consciousness . . . recommended for wide purchase." — *Library Journal*

" . . . the best manual for our 'hard times' . . . " — *Saturday Review*. $5.00 ($12.50 cloth).

The Federal Budget
and Social Reconstruction
Marcus Raskin, Editor

This study describes the Federal Budget, sets new priorities for government spending and presents alternative policies for defense, energy, health and taxation.

"The issuance of this report is a major political event and a challenge to mainstream ideology. It should be widely purchased."—*Library Journal*

" . . . a first-rate critique of the present economic crisis in this country . . . a valuable blueprint for charting a more humane and just society for all Americans in future years."—James Abourezk. $8.95.

Postage and Handling:
All orders must be prepaid. For delivery within the USA, please add 15% of order total. For delivery outside the USA, add 20%. Standard discounts available upon request.

Please write the Institute for Policy Studies, 1901 Que Street, N.W., Washington, D.C. 20009 for our complete catalog of publications and films.